GROWING UP, THEN THINGS FAILED

How did She Acquired Strength

RHONDA MAXINE BOGGI

CITIOFBOOKS, INC.
3736 Eubank NE Suite A1
Albuquerque, NM 87111-3579
www.citiofbooks.com
Hotline: 1 (877) 389-2759
Fax: 1 (505) 930-7244

Ordering Information:
Quantity sales. Special discounts are available on quantity purchases by corporations, associations, and others. For details, contact the publisher at the address above.

Printed in the United States of America.

ISBN-13:   Softcover   979-8-90124-154-7
             eBook   979-8-90124-155-4

Library of Congress Control Number: 2026906274

Dedication

To all the people whose love and endless support built my strength: to my late parents - Percy and Verilyn Farley for your endured genes, my faithful siblings, extended family, close relatives, and kind friends who never give up on me.

God's gifts in my life:

Mary, Melanie, Benjamin, and Seth,

You are the best thing that ever happened to me.

To his honor, Josh, who promised to love and cherish me in good and bad times,

And finally, Glory be to God, who holds my future in the palm of his hands.

Acknowledgements

As in everything I have done in my life, I will first thank God for His love and guidance, giving me the strength to complete this memoir. All of this would not be possible if I did not receive the love, support, and encouragement from the close people in my life.

I am beyond grateful for the life that my late parents, Father Percy Samuel Farley and Verilyn Maxine Farley, gave to me. Dad, your guidance shaped me into the woman I am today. You always believed in me, pushed me to educate myself, and always kept on teaching me. You did not live long enough to see the product of your teachings – you went from this world too soon. You always wanted me to be a doctor, and I did this for you.

Mom, your endless love and devotion for me never withered. You gave up your sleep and put my needs before yours by sitting next to me and ensuring that my early education was built on a solid foundation. Your endless love for your family and always giving your all has transferred into my own heart.

To my very wise stepmother, Sister Carol, thanks for opening and creating a special place in your heart for us. Since the time I met you, your love has remained unconditional. You have listened to me and guided me while appreciating me all the time. You cooked and would freeze food for me, apart from making the best soup that gave me strength when I was malnourished.

I would not have been standing as proud as I am today without the determination and persistence of my daughter, Mary Maxine Joseph.

She, on a day-to-day basis, motivated me to complete this book. She offered her assistance with the younger ones so that I could focus on writing. Mary, I have felt so tired and drained on many occasions, but you always encouraged me. You pushed me into meeting deadlines and persuaded me when I could not convince myself.

My daughter, Melanie Aleshia Joseph, you have proven yourself to be as independent as possible, ensuring you work hard on your assessments. You would always find a way to secure your ride to and from the various school activities while allowing me time to excuse myself from showing up on time for your games. You would often peep your head into the room and ask me if I was working on my book. I am aware that you wanted me to complete this memoir, even if that meant focusing less on my business.

My two little boys, Benjamin and Seth, thank you for excusing my absence whenever I locked myself in a room to write this memoir or distracted you with your favorite gadgets or television programs so that I could work on my book. Sometimes, you did not even understand why I allowed you to use all my computer papers to draw or write, but you kept yourself occupied with them regardless.

My husband, Josh Boggi, my best friend, partner, and dedicated husband for almost six years: thank you for your unmovable and unconditional love and support since the time I met you. You ensured that all the bills were paid on time and that our family never ran out of supplies. Thanks for sneaking in my computer to correct a line or two and construct the sentences correctly. My Sister, Desa Kay: I am so grateful for your love. You and your family have also been there for us in good times and sickness. You have demonstrated your unconditional love and support for my family when I have not been around or feeling strong enough to care for them. Putting your job on the side, you ensured that my little ones were protected, and for that, I will forever be grateful. You set your job aside to ensure that my little ones were protected. One of the best things to ever happen to me is your migration to this country.

To my niece, Keanna, and nephews, Noel, especially Keron and

Keon: you all rock! Thank you so much for your free babysitting services and the unconditional love you have shown to my boys. You always teach them how to play basketball and other indoor games. Not just that, but you have given them your expensive phones to play, skipping your favorite television programs to put theirs, just to ensure they are kept quiet.

To the other nieces and nephews: your love and support throughout the years have been unmeasurable. Kevon and Melissa Farley, thank you for constantly babysitting and pampering my little boys whenever I take a trip to my home country. Most importantly, my niece, Mother Odiaha Coxall, thank you for giving up your job and temporarily leaving the love of your life to lend me a helping hand. You ensured my little boys were also clean, happy, and safe. I greatly admire your qualities at this young age. To my elder brother, Dexter Farley: thanks for your weekly check-ins, especially when things were not going my way. You have proven to be an exemplar for the best brother I could have. You often opened your home to welcome my family and me, even with unannounced visits or whenever I wanted a getaway. I will always be grateful for your dedication to your family.

I could not complete this memoir without mentioning my other siblings, Marrell Farley and Donnette Farley. Thank you for your unconditional love whether you visit or I visit. Our closets and food pantry would not have been functional without your presence. Heartiest thanks to my dearest sister, Marrell, for ensuring my freezer has ready-to-cook meats and fish. You ensured that I was stocked up on food for two months, making my busy schedule manageable.

Without my family, I would not function successfully as an employee and as a mother. My other brothers, Trevoun and Junior Percy Farley, thank you for ensuring that my trips are safe and we have our favorite food and fruits ready.

To my late brother, Pastor Okechi Farley, thanks for all your prayers, scripture verses, spiritual food and nourishment, and encouragement at the beginning of every year. Your help was eloquent, extraordinary, and created spiritual growth that set my goals for the upcoming years.

I will re-read some of these scriptures each year while reflecting on your presence.

Thanks to my aunts, especially Nadine, for showing me your motherly love in the absence of your sister. You always answered the ring of your phone and lent me a shoulder whenever I needed it. You listened to my tearful voice, offering your mature and experiential guidance to make me feel better.

As for my in-laws, I want to especially thank Harriet Boggi for warmly welcoming my girls and me into your family and offering us your tender care. You ensured that our feet were always above the ground and that our well-being stayed afloat. You often left your busy schedule to book a flight to ensure that you gave us your helping hands in times of need. You research well and always make sure that our well-being is based on profound facts, even at a distance. You offered us your mature and brilliant knowledge when ours was weak. Thanks for all the guidance, for being present in a powerful way, and for caring for my little boys. Special thanks for ensuring that my thesis was corrected on time to secure my graduation.

Thanks to my former in-laws for providing me with your love. You have ensured that my older girls were cared for. Not just that, you have gone above and beyond to safeguard their needs and prioritize their education. Your prayers, then, were appreciated and protected us during those stormy days.

My present in-laws: you rock! Thanks for the acknowledgment and support you have given to my family and me in good and bad times.

Next, my incredible friends, especially the closer ones, Nuci, Omega, Megan, V, and Carla, thank you for always being there for me. Whether in hospital beds or emergency rooms, Nuci provided me with her steadfast support, sitting in a chair for long hours as she left her love behind to ensure that I was safe and sound. You nursed me back to health by your frequent check-in and meals delivery. Carla, you cooked trays and varieties of food to ensure that my family was fed while I was busy with my education. When I was new to this country, you gave me a job by handing over your patients so I could put food on my table. You took me shopping and told me about all the quality and cost-effective stores, simultaneously stimulating my home décor skills.

Omega, each year you have brought your organic produce and chicken from Canada and drove the scary roads in New York to come to me, whether you gave me company for even an hour. Your weekly check-ins by text, messages, and phone calls mean a great deal to me and will never go unrecognized.

To another incredible friend, Megan, thank you for pulling out the best in me and reminding me to use what I have when I did not recognize it myself or ever knew it existed. You ensured my advanced knowledge was always utilized by stimulating and steering my entrepreneurial skills. When I thought higher education was the answer and expressed thoughts of seeking more knowledge, you pushed me to explore and initiate my own business. You ensured your help, walking me along the path of being a business owner by seeking out the various channels from which I could attain guidance.

Thanks to my friend, V, for you have created a balance between my former family affairs and ensuring my well-being. You have led me into making some of the most challenging life decisions. Additionally, you applauded me for my strength and supported some of my choices. Most importantly, thanks for extending your love to my children, giving them a sense of belonging when they felt alone. You also guided me during my search for different business opportunities, for which I am grateful. Thank you for never separating yourself from me even after my former love life and family crumbled.

To the other amazing friends, you stood by me through thick and thin. When I was sad, you shared laughter. When I was bored, you have enlightened me. When I felt trapped, you took me for dinner, and when I was down, you uplifted my spirit and reminded me that there is hope.

To the unforgettable and incredible Lenore, your name has been mentioned with every step in my career advancement. You believed in me when I had doubts. I remember when you persuaded me to seek higher education even when I told you that my brain was fried from all the studying. When I did not understand the educational system in the US, you took that time and placed all the phone calls, even scribbling my initial admission letter.

I have to mention my prayer-warrior friend, Tyana, for always being by my side. She often dreamt about the events in my life before they even occurred, putting me on my guard; I would not even believe some of that before it happened. Tyana was one of my former students and the Director of Activities in New Jersey at the first building where I started working as a nurse practitioner. She immediately opened her office, cleared a part of her desk, and shared with me when I did not even have a chair to sit on. She and her staff ensured that I was always comfortable and well-fed.

I must applaud my friend Nicky for all her devoted time, getting my hair looking spectacular. You came home from work and raced to the hair store before it closed so that you were ready for me when I popped into your house any time of the day. You made it look so easy, providing a set of ears even when you are tired. I will never forget the beautiful conversations we shared as we passed the time. You also opened your doors and allowed my little one to disrupt your expensive décor while working on my hair to ensure that I look sharp.

A special thank you to Matron B and one of my elder cousins Keith and his beautiful wife, Rosie, for housing me without a price while I started on my career path as a nurse. You embraced me with your love and kindness in my time of need.

Thank you, pastor, for always being there promptly when I need spiritual healing. At the sound of the phone ringing, my pastor always picked up and offered his encouragement along with his presence. Thank you for always supporting me and healing me through the scriptures of God.

To my beautiful Godmother, thank you for your countless support. As a child, you babysat me while my parents were not there, protected me from danger, ensured that I was clean, well-fed, and showered me with numerous gifts. You continued to provide support and encouragement while praying for my family and me to date.

A special thanks to all my former and current United Health bosses for your support. You stimulated my professional growth by critiquing my job performance and helping me become a quality leader. You also recognized, rewarded my advancements, and welcomed my ideas without turning me away. Additionally, you allowed me the flexibility to create a balance while I advanced my education and built my family.

To all my former students, thanks for believing in me. You persuaded me to write this memoir even when I had doubts, believing that my numerous inspiring stories would influence and heal many. You were open to me and accepted my tool kit on the restoration of hope and my resilience with open arms.

When Rhonda Maxine Boggi nee Farley was growing up and living the Christian faith according to the Bible, she had a dream. She wanted to enjoy and share her life with one partner while following the rites of Christianity. She hoped that the man she marries in her life would become her Prince Charming and wanted to be surrounded by his family, who would thoroughly love her.

Rhonda's journey in life was filled with many obstacles. The most wounding for her was the willful yet destructive act that forced her to break the bonds with the man she believed to be the love of her life. Bidding her marriage, a farewell due to her husband being involved in extramarital affairs while shattering her personality, she was left with a bitter taste in her mouth.

The end of that marriage left a physical and psychological effect on her girls and almost left Rhonda with chronic depression. She began to interrogate her spiritual convictions while searching for direction in life.

Nevertheless, despite all the brawls in her life, she overcame and prospered with amusing bravery. How did Rhonda gain her strength?

This memoir is evidence that distinguishes the embodiment of true love when you are in a relationship. It is written to bring courage to all suffering or who have suffered from broken relationships, hoping to nourish and strengthen the readers.

Additionally, I hope this will become a must-read and a foundation, especially for girls as young as ones in 5th grade, as an added course curriculum called life lesson.

To all my readers, life may be a fairytale but does not always remain one.

About the Author

Rhonda Maxine Boggi nee Farley grew up and lived the Christian faith according to the bible. She had the greatest dream of enjoying and sharing her life with one life partner as a part of her Christianity. She meets and hopes the man she married initially was her prince charming and believed to be surrounded by his family who thoroughly loves her. Life's journey for Rhonda was filled with many obstacles. The most obnoxious was the willful destructive act that forced her to break the strong bonds with the man she believed to be the love of her life. The farewell of her marriage due to extramarital affairs and the attempts to destroy her persona left a bitter taste in the relationship she thinks she had built with most of Joseph's family.

The end of that marriage created physical and psychological effects for our girls and almost left Rhonda with chronic mental health struggles. Relentlessly, Rhonda began to interrogate her spiritual conviction and others'.

Nevertheless, despite all the brawls in her life, with pensive bravery, she overcame and prospers. How did Rhonda gain her strength?

This memoir is evidence that distinguishes the embodiment of true love only when you are in a relationship. The hope is tobring courage for all suffering from broken relationships and will nourish and strengthen the readers.

Preface

October 2020

During my childhood, I had dreams in which I was planning my future, working hard to accomplish my goals. **They were about** becoming a doctor, having an affectionate husband and children, and traveling the world. During a vacation to the city at my grandmother's, I shared with my aunt how I dreamed of living in huge homes next to each other, and sharing supplies willingly, which would include shoes, clothing, and bags. During those days, my teachers, parents, and other elders in the village had one unique question: they would ask every little boy and girl, and to date, that question still hangs around. It was that question that kept me on track as I journeyed through life and ensured that my answer fulfilled its purpose. The famous question was, "What do you want to be when you grow up?" My response was simple: "I wanted to become a doctor."

As a child, I often saw how my family members, neighbors, and other individuals surrounding me were sick; and how my caring hands could be beneficial. I was too small to care for them at the time, so in turn, I mimicked that care while role-playing dollhouse with my siblings and at times my neighbors.

I enjoyed feelings of being thought of admirably because of such an ambitious and prestigious career field ahead of me, one of becoming a doctor. I was looking forward to the day when I would be caring for my brothers, sisters, little cousins, and any neighbors and the population at large, helping those in need. This caring capability was so deeply rooted in my brain that I would go as far as expressing it by using pigeon peas as medicine, shaping tipped limbs from the trees to give injections, and tearing old clothing to use as cling to wrap some pretend-to-be wounds. Even my dad instilled these thoughts in me and encouraged me that I should become a doctor.

So far in my life, I've obtained a doctoral degree in nursing. I am a faculty, an educator, a mentor, a clinical advisor, a preceptor, a registered nurse, and a nurse practitioner. I have worked two jobs and am living the American dream while raising a family. I have sat in many classrooms, some of which I fell asleep in and was woken by my colleagues. But then the remainder of my resting hours at nights, I would make it seem like a day to ensure I've attained an education as a black working-class American woman. This started after one of my colleagues encouraged me to go back to school, assuring me that I could do well. She held my hands and led me back to obtain my bachelor's degree. I had doubts then but later learned that anything could be achieved in life if you work hard for it.

Being raised in the Christian faith, I also remembered my duties under the Bible. I faithfully attended church and participated in some minor church programs and events as well. Some Sundays, I was not in the church due to work and doing my clinical requirements for school. But still, I always prayed and asked God to arrange a job for me in which my Sundays were free, and I could fulfill my divine obligations. I feel blessed, knowing that although I am busy, I still find the time for fellowship and spend time praising and serving God.

I have held many positions and titles along my career voyage. I have sat with people of different colors, different races, beliefs, and political affiliations. I struggled as a young black woman, trying to fit in many rooms as I exerted my passion. I admit it was quite difficult to work with people who were snakes, backstabbers, and those who would undermine me, saying I was too young to hold some titles. Nevertheless, I held on to the values that were instilled in me since the day I was born; to love humanity, get along, and work with people regardless of their class, creed, and culture, and treat everyone equally. I never allow room for other behaviors to prevail over my passion.

When I became a nurse, I strictly followed the imagery of the late Florence Nightingale, who was known to be "The Lady with the Lamp." I've looked up to her since she was the pioneer and the foundational philosopher for modern nursing. After I repeated the pledge daily during my days of training at our morning devotions, I aspired to be like her as she was an elevator to the nursing profession. I was taught how to be humble, dignified, caring, and compassionate in all that I would do for humanity. But, during the start of my career, I faced many backlashes. I have been misjudged, accused, misinterpreted, and misperceived by others for unsure reasons. I was invited for scheduled interviews for many titles and positions, even just a day before the interview, to be on time. And as I showed up, I was turned away with a confused facial expression and soft voice echoing, "that position is no longer available."

Since entering the career as a nurse, the public eyes have viewed me differently. Society was taught that a person who is dressed in an all-white uniform is respectable and honorable. On rainy days, as I traveled to the nursing school, instead of walking that long distance from the Stelling Road to Cowdam, where my nursing classroom was located, I was offered free rides without paying for transportation. My white uniform continued to stay white; my nursing shoes looked as though they were right out of the box. Not always did I have to travel from home to the nursing school, but sometimes I also stayed at one of my elder cousin KM's, who willingly accepted me into his one-bedroom home at that time. He co-parented me together with his wife RM without a cost. Their home was filled with love, laughter, and a balance between pleasure and Christianity. When he returned home after working on the sea, I stayed at one of my colleagues, who was the Matron's daughter that later became sister-in-law LB. Matron was very humble. She accepted me and nurtured me without any cost. Her entire family adopted me well; they showed me much love and respect while Matron cooked and ensured that my meals are packed for school the next day, and I don't have to stay hungry.

When I arrived in America, I did not understand the process or the procedure of obtaining my RN degree. A former coworker from Guyana CG, who later became like a sister to me, offered me my first job with one of her private patients. During this time, she walked me through how to obtain credentialing to sit for the licensed practical nursing boards.

My former mother-in-law was also gracious enough to get me my second job as a dental assistant, after knowing and working alongside a dentist and a beautiful, well-dressed dental assistant (from Denserv) at her facility called 'Green Park Nursing Home.' I worked at various facilities, one to three days of the week when the job opening was available.

I later sat for the LPN boards and got successful, then started working at the said facility as my formal mother-in-law. While working at that facility, I also met a Guyanese nurse, a licensed practical nurse (LPN), who was studying for his registered nursing (RN) program. He offered me materials and showed me the process of how to sit for my registered professional nursing boards. The process was lengthy but gave me enough time to study and be successful - I did surpass all his expectations and mine.

I remembered that day vividly when the mailman gave me a piece of slip to go to the post office to obtain a package. I received my nursing license in the big white firmed envelope, but at the time, I did not know what was inside and what to expect. I could hardly wait to reach home so that I could finally rip open that white envelope and check whatever was inside. As I pulled out the first piece of paper, I noticed my licensed practical nursing certification, and I was surprised beyond my wits. I rejoiced, cried, and later celebrated my life dream come true. I was astonished for a bit that I was successful at the exam, even though I was not too acquainted with the nursing education in America, along with the roadblock I faced during preparation for the board exam.

The next step was applying for the RN license. I used the materials that were given to me by the Guyanese LPN and began studying night after night and even extended hours during the day. When I thought that I knew most of the material and would pass, I fixed a date to sit for that RN board and took the exam.

Before my results were completed, I was called by surprise by the nursing director. I was scared to enter her office at first, as I was afraid that I must've mishandled a situation that occurred on the unit that I was working on, and she must've called me for it. I was dumbfounded as I sat down with mixed feelings, my heart palpitating; the first thing she asked me was how I was doing. She then proceeded to tell me about all the great things she had heard of my performances. Her following sentence offered me a position to work full-time as a nursing supervisor at the facility. She perhaps checked online and must've seen that I was successful at the exam.

I told her that I took the boards three days ago and I am waiting on my results. She then told me that I have to bring it to her as soon as I obtained my nursing license. That said day, I reached home, and the license was there waiting for me. I took it in the very next day. The Director of nursing told me to wear regular clothes and a lab coat to start training the next day as a registered nursing supervisor.

I was terrified initially since I was only 23 years of age and was overseeing the management of about 400 residents and 100 older nursing staff on the various shifts. I was given this position because of my skills and my willingness to assist on the unit, ensure that the residents were cared for, and show the representation of a good leader while working as a licensed practical nurse. However, after supervising employees for a while and repeating the same tasks day by day, I became bored and decided to seek a job at a hospital. During that time, I was not picky at all. I was ready to accept a job in a hospital at any department since it was difficult to get a job at hospitals then. I was called in to be interviewed for a part-time position at a hospital for joint disease.

In the interview process, the unit manager loved my spirits and passion for nursing; and she decided to offer me a full-time position, overseeing the chronic pain management program on the 4-12 shift. I happily accepted that job, then changed my status at the nursing home from full-time to part-time. During this time, I was skeptical about working in a hospital since many hospitals were merging, downsizing, and or closing, and I also had a new commitment as a first-time homebuyer.

While working at the nursing home, it taught me one lesson, which is "how to blow where the wind carries you." For sure, I understood how to manage the residents, and doctors viewed me as an independent nurse who knew how to manage acute and chronic diseases. At times when I would call the doctors to report a change in condition, they would jokingly say, "You know what to do. Why are you calling me?"

This inspired and motivated my yearning for higher education and the quest for being autonomous. I continued working a full-time and a part-time job while I sought my undergraduate degree. I then registered and stepped my feet in the door, proceeded to sit in the chair to take my first class in America. Even though I wanted to go back to school from the beginning, I did not understand the process, so I procrastinated. One quiet evening, while working at the hospital on the 4 to 12 shift, one of my team members, LD, embraced me and asked me why I was wasting my time there when I could have been in school and used some of this time to do my assignment. Although I decided to go back to school eventually, I was still having second thoughts and even told LD that I thought I was too old. I felt that my brain cells wouldn't work the same as before; they might be clogged, and I may not remember studying and writing papers.

However, to start, I decided to register for one class, and in the end, I realized that I had scored an A. This motivated me to take two additional courses that semester in which I obtained two additional A(s). I was surprise at how I could still focus and study like before. But what I learned from this experience is that if you are motivated enough, you can accomplish anything you set forth on. I did well, and I was placed on the dean's list and graduated with honors. I then attained my first degree in America, a bachelor's degree in health care administration/health care management.

When I think back on it, it was quite unusual how I could climb the clinical ladder so rapidly; from working as a dental assistant to a nursing supervisor. However, his movement created a lot of friction in the nursing home environment for some senior nurses. They once applied for the position as a nursing supervisor but were jealous of my success. They called me names, and, well, I did make a few enemies.

These moments allowed me to grow professionally and individually while reflecting on my past and paved the way for my future endeavors. I was humbled as I dispensed my duties diligently and with confidence. This path also allowed me to sit in the shoes of an evening nursing supervisor and, at times, also an administrator. This was done fiercely and thoroughly and also provided me with more excellent opportunities ahead.

TABLE OF CONTENT

CHAPTER 1:
While Growing

I can remember spending most of my childhood attending church, listening to gospel music, reading my Bible, and praying to God. Going to church was the only option. We were forbidden from going to parties or movies. It was difficult to get the time to go to church, as we often must ensure that our chores are done. Some of which involved going to the farm, watering the garden, harvesting large baskets of vegetables, and making sure that they were clean and ready for the markets the next day. One of the most time-consuming events was the picking and shelling of pigeon peas, which took almost 5 to 8 hours, depending on the amount being harvested. My youth group team at church was very caring and helpful. They offered a great helping hand. This secured our chances of getting that Friday night to assemble for the fellowship in the church weekly youth group.

I rarely attended Sunday school in the mornings since I had many chores to complete on the farm. At times, one of the sisters in the church would hold Sunday school classes in the afternoon at a different location, approximately 1.5 miles walking distance at the bottom of a private house. I enjoyed singing Sunday school songs, more so when I was chosen to be one of the leaders singing.

One of the choruses I sang was *God, love is like a circle*, a circle that is big and round, and when we have a circle, no end can be found, so the love of Jesus goes on to eternity. Forever and forever, I know that God loves me. I also remember reciting scripture verses that were required each week at the Sunday school. If I did not remember my given verse to recite, I often chose an easier one from the Bible (remember Lots Wife) or (Jesus Weep). One of my favorite stories in the Bible was *David and the lion*. I did not have a huge Bible to take to Sunday school, but I took a little Testament. As the offering was being collected at the Sunday school, I was embarrassed as I had none to offer. Whenever I got a coin, I would save it for Sunday school rather than buy candy as my other siblings chose. I always thought that God knows my heart (the willingness and cheer to the giver).

Youth group itself was fun since you met with other youths to learn the Bible together. The Bible was understood in a playful manner which brought laughter and fun. There were banquets, youth rallies, and youth fairs that took place at our mother church. I did not get the chance to visit the mother church often; my parents did not want to spend extra money. Likewise, I did not have "the appropriate attire," as my parents would say. It bothers me at times, but I could not complain.

Practicing for the Christmas concert and harvest was fun. As much as I could not sing a solo, I was invited to sing in the choir. For the most part, I would do poetry and act in skits. I also remembered when I would accompany the elders and youth group to go caroling at Christmas. In those days, the music was melodic; we sang the well-known Christmas carols while the drum beat loudly, and we danced along the street, going from house to house. We took turns shaking the tambourine. The homes were so peaceful and festive with the fragrance of black cake, pepper pot, and freshly baked bread (some of my festive foods) that they made me feel hungry. Christmas dinner at church itself was a big well-to-do; I often looked forward to that opportunity to wear my best gown (although not as fancy as today). In my mind, I was getting ready for a Grammy award. To me, dressing up fancy and stepping into the beautifully decorated hall at the church entrance was the Hollywood feel. The table I sat at was chosen by the committee, fancy with festive color, the atmosphere filled with Christmas aromas. The meals were expensive and delicious, and the soft Christmas was reclusive to the atmosphere, which made me feel glamorous.

We moved from one house to another in my earlier childhood because my dad was a police officer and was stationed in various places. We moved from number three village West Coast Berbice to number 10 village West Coast Berbice. At number three, one of the memories was spending time with my godmother, who lived obliquely opposite my house. I glanced at one picture and noticed that I was dressed in a yellow, green, and white gabardine material pant-suit with my hair scattered all over my head in an afro. Of course, my older sister and I were dressed alike as though we were twins. Visiting my godmother was fun as I looked forward to the gifts and love she showered me with. I would play with her dog, even though I feared her. She named her Sabrina.

My godmother's blue house was inward from the road; I remembered running from the gate to the bottom of the house. My godmother would then give me a bath then feed me with a peanut butter sandwich. The peanut butter was crunchy. Even today, I do not eat peanut butter because it makes me feel so nauseous. I also used to look forward to my birthday and Christmas since I was sure that she had a gift waiting for me.

While I was living at the number 10 village West Coast Berbice, I attended number eight nursery school. For a short period at the school, I made friends with whom I was not in contact. Those days, I sat on my father's motorcycle packed with four of my other siblings going to number eight primary school. Once my foot touched the exhaust, it got burned. My dad had yelled, "Get *a sense, why did you put your foot there.*"

Another silly thing I did was touch pepper seeds that my father had put on a zinc sheet in the sun to dry for replanting. After playing with the pepper seeds, I rubbed my eyes with my hands. I saw the moon and stars; my entire face was swollen and burned. My mother decided to wash it with sweetened water (sugar water). That was my worst nightmare.

Those days, safety was far from becoming. I was standing in the middle of the road with my two hands in the air, stopping all the passing vehicles. I am not sure where I was going or why, but thank God I was ignored by the passing vehicles. Until one of my caring neighbors chased me off the road then reported this occurrence to my parents. That report spiked a good whipping, through which I did learn the right from the wrong.

We then finally moved to number four village where I spent most of my childhood growing. Our house was partly completed, halfway floored, and the windows were covered with clear white plastic and salt bags until my parents had enough money to have it finished. Those days were scary, but I had to be content with what my parents could afford as a kid. My father placed huge pieces of furniture to block the unfinished flooring so that we did not accidentally fall through.

One of my childhood friends was ML: she used to walk north to wait for me after lunch to walk with me to our school in the south (number five primary school). During this time, we stopped at her grandfather's snack shop, which she would play that she was changing a quarter, and she picked up approximately one dollar in coins. ML shared those coins with me. While in school, I felt rich, as I had a lot of money to buy snacks. Some of the snacks I enjoyed then were ice pops, Flutie, Mathai, and chicken foot, with plenty sour.

Going to school late was sometimes beyond my control. I walked home from school for lunch; at times, lunch was not ready because my parents had to wait on the fish vendor to buy fish to cook; this sometimes ran late. My teachers did not take that as an excuse; therefore, I suffered the consequences by going to detention, which involved cleaning the schoolyard, getting lashes in my hands with a wild cane, and the humiliation of staying in a separate line. My responsibilities as a school child were to ensure that my nails were always clean, trimmed, and my teeth brushed, and my mouth free of odor. In addition, I must wear clean clothes.

To combat the humiliation or prevent myself from being singled out, I often told my mother that I preferred to eat the cooked white rice with sugar, milk, or butter. At times, I would ask for a snack instead of a meal. My mother did not want me to eat this; she believed in a healthy meal. After the meal was finished, I used to race down the road with my thin bowed legs. I could not enjoy those meals since I had to rush through them so fast. I had to please both my mother and my teacher.

My teacher would go around the class and hit the students on their hands with a ruler if their nails were dirty. So, I would quickly check mine. If they were too long, I'd quickly bite mine on the way to school. The chores before school, such as sweeping the yard, sometimes caused the dust to fasten itself underneath my nails. I was not that privileged to have a nail clipper, and sometimes, I could hardly find a razor blade to cut them. And when I did, it would often be too sharp that I used to cut my skin or too dull to clip my nails.

I never enjoyed listening to the radio (broadcast for school) since I was mostly tired. I did not like the radio announcer's voice. At the end of this session, my teacher would question me pertaining to the subject discussed. As I scored an answer incorrectly, I received two whiplashes on my palm. This forced me to pay close attention and enhance my listening capabilities.

CHAPTER 2:

While Growing The farm

I grew up on a huge farm located just behind our house and stretches to the sea dam. My dad planted mixed varieties of vegetable-and fruit trees. Those days, I spent every weekend and most holidays on the farm weeding, watering the garden, and harvesting for the market the next day. I had a machete assigned to me, whereas, on school days, I spent the early mornings and evenings watering the garden and reaping the crops, and at times, taking them to the market before school. As I weed the assigned area, my father would come and check to see if I cut the weeds from the roots. If I did the job halfway, I would have to go back and redo it.

For that, I disliked weekends and school closures. There was no time to go on vacation, as the vacation was spent on the farm. I despise the times when my dad asked us to pack the pots and utensils to go on the farm because that meant we would be spending the entire day until the night. During this time, I rested in a coconut tree-branch tent with blankets and sheets placed on the floor, or we took turns to sleep in the hammock. I did appreciate nature and the fresh sea breeze pouring in. As I prepared lunch, my dad would ensure the pots were filled with vegetables and, at times, a blend of vegetables.

We had customers who would often come to the house early to buy a small portion of vegetables. My father would send me to the farm to reap their crops. I did pick and offered extra portions as they cried and shared their burden of how many kids, they must feed with a bit of money to spend. I may give additional fruits to assist but hid that from my father. Sometimes, I add some eggs or two pieces of dried fish.

I hated fetching two buckets of water in my hands and sometimes on my head to water the garden. This occurred daily, before or after school, unless it rained. To combat this, I would mix the salty seawater with the piped water to water the plants. The majority of times, this kills the plants. I suffered corns on both hands from those buckets that did not have a padded handle. I choose to carry both buckets the said times to decrease the multiple trips and lessen the time to get this job done.

I also reaped and carried huge piles of vegetables on my head and got them ready for market the same or the next day. Additionally, huge bunches of bananas, baskets of okras, long beans, and tomatoes were also included. I hated reaping callaloo; this was time-consuming to prepare; they were sandy and had to be properly prepared. I wore long socks in gloves to reap the hot peppers and the small rounded shaped by the bucket filled to the top. During the walk from the farm to the house, I smelled the hot fragrance of hot peppers. I had to be careful that I did not touch my eyes or face as I did not want to suffer the consequences. My father ensured that all his produce was well prep and cleanly presented to the market.

Sometimes, I would have to go to the markets to sell the vegetables before school and sometimes walked the streets in the Indian villages. As much as I hated it, I had to follow the instructions from my parents. During school days, I could wholesale vegetables and sometimes offer extra so that I can finish quickly and be ready for school on time.

I was terrified of going to the market at first since none of my peers did, and if they accompanied their parents during the weekends, I hid from them. My brother did not understand why I pushed him to sell. I always brushed it off by saying they know you better. When the market is closed, I'd take the vegetables to Hopetown Village West Coast Berbice to market them. Being so young, I did not have the marketing skills that were needed. Often, one of the elders in the market would assist me in the pricing. I would sometimes repay her with some vegetables to show my appreciation.

Not only at the market, at times, but I also had to walk the street going from house to house with innumerable sized baskets of harvested produce or mangoes. I was humiliated shouting "Mangoes, Mangoes" to "Get your fresh produce here." These chairs were all taken care of before school. My father would allow us to spend any of our earnings to buy food if I was hungry. The produces vended fast; they were fresh and reasonably priced; I did not have to worry about going to school late.

The fish pond

Not only a farm, but we also had a fishpond at the back of our house, which consisted of (tilapias and Hassa). Although I liked and enjoyed fishing, I hated cleaning the tilapias. As you clean this kind of live fish, their fins are stuck into your fingers and cause them to burn if not held correctly. Therefore, when my dad bought or caught these fishes in large amounts, I would sometimes give one of my neighbors to help me clean them and pay her a small amount in return.

One rainy day, my mother took my little sister to her clinic appointment. I decided to go into this fishpond that was about half-filled with water covering my waistline depth. I did not see the danger then, I just wanted to have fun while trying to imitate other swimmers. My mom unexpectedly came home earlier than expected, and I was caught in the pond trying to swim. My older sister was wiser. She quickly got out, rushed into the bathroom, and began bathing; she had her clothing and water prepared. Oh boy, I got some lashes from her to remind me about the danger of this pond.

From the same pond, I would also dig some mud from its side and use it to reface our mud-baking oven and fire-wood cooking stove weekly and polish it once during the week. This mud provided a smooth coating of clay that enhanced our clay and wood-burning appliances that we cooked and backed on during the non-rainy days. This itself was difficult to cook with initially, as I had to ensure that the wood was dried and adequate amounts were available to complete the meal. I sometimes mixed the wood with dried coconuts shells to ensure the dog's food was cooked, and fine rice was boiled to feed the pigs.

CHAPTER 3:
My home

In the latter part of my childhood, I grew up in a four-bedroom house in a huge yard in which the house was built about 90 feet from the road. The front of the yard had enough space to play outdoor games with my siblings; my parents did not allow us to go to the ballfield or any of the neighbors' places to play. However, the neighborhood children were allowed in our yard. We played various games, including circle tennis, one-two-three red light, and hopscotch. I remember taking long jumps with my bowed legs in the remaining emptied box to score a "baby."

I enjoyed the family time as my father roasted corn, and we played "which hand" and "cock and juice." Cock meant one, and juice meant two. I would lose most of the time since I did not catch on to his tricks to drop one if someone said, "juice." As kids, we did not think of germs as the corn passed from hand to hand while we ate it. During those days, my dad also told us scary stories. When lights were switched off, we imagined shadows to be the spirits of the dead bodies, felt scared, and cried aloud.

Other enjoyable memories were surrounding the Christmas holidays. We prepared for Christmas by scrubbing the walls, painting the tree's trunks white, cleaning all the elegant dishes and delicate pieces of China in the cabinet, and making sure that the yard was free of weeds and looked spotless. Even though it may not rain, I had to wear long black boots and pick up the leaves. Although it rained, the yard had to be kept clean. Therefore, I had to wear long boots. Our yard was always immaculate, as my father made sure to disseminate his military qualities to his environment.

My father also slaughtered pigs, ducks, and chickens as we had a huge clientele for that. We often received numerous orders; he marketed more pigs than he had actually planned. I assisted him by holding the legs of the pigs while he prepared them. His meats were well prepared and marketed fast.

I was not of the age to join the church group going around the neighborhood to sing carols. Instead, I enjoyed that era of waking up in the middle of the night as the church members would come around beating the drums and singing melodious carols. This emulsified the spirit and gave me the true meaning of Christmas. My family was engaged in the local tradition of Christmas meals, but no gifts were placed under the Christmas tree; the lights were colorful and bright. I did not partake in the other ethnic holidays but speedily ran to the roadside to see the floats exhibition drown the road.

CHAPTER 4:
The Faith

I attended one of the Full Gospel and the Assembly of God churches in the next villages. There, I learned about the Bible and got excited after reading about the miracles of God. These miracles and stories made me convert into a more dedicated Christian.

I was nine years old when I was water baptized and became a member of the said church. There I was practicing the faith that I had in my religion and was learning the Bible. Another reason for doing so was to escape home and to be in the fame of socialization.

I got to learn so much about Christianity there. I was enlightened by the words of God and the promises he had made to his people in the Bible. He showed me vision through a phrase written in the Bible, which said, "I hold your future in the palm of my hands, I will never leave you nor forsake, but will be with you until the end." These words of God gave me hope. They gave me the courage and assured me that God would be with me in the toughest of times. Even if I sinned, I would quickly go down on my knees and beg God for forgiveness. He never leaves your side, especially in tough and struggling times, and this divine faith and inner composure help you hold on to those promises of God.

It was difficult for me to practice Christianity with all my heart at such a tender age, and that too while being surrounded by people and temptations. My concentration span was so affected that I wasn't able to concentrate on my prayers and whether it was my dad playing music or the reverberating beats of the music being played next door would interfere with my thoughts.

The Pastor at my church was very stringent about believers living the biblical ways. He wanted all the church visitors to come in proper attire in accordance with the code of conduct and attire set by religion. I was not allowed to adorn myself in a male's garments, nor was I allowed to wear any jewelry or makeup.

I kept friends only at the church since my school friends were dreadful, leading me awry. I was very close to my church friends, and I enjoyed attending youth groups and socializing with my fellow brothers and sisters in the church.

Learning the Bible was done in a fun way to celebrate birthdays, and convincing my parents to go away to youth convention was a great deal. My first trip away was truly amazing as I felt the presence of God there and also met many young Christian boys and girls. What made me happier was the interest these little girls and boys had in Christianity and how all of us shared God's miracles with each other. It was quite enlightening and uplifting to share the word of God amongst ourselves.

I would say that it was a wonderful feeling as I was connecting with the lovely people of God. I will always cherish those memories, and the care, and protection from the elders, while I was having fellowship with Godly people, the youths. I am really glad that the event went really well and everything happened as per the plan.

This brings me to an incident that happened one fine early bloomy morning in August while I was cleaning the yard with a little "hard broom." I was almost blustered when my former Pastor O approached and asked me if I would consider getting married to one of the youth leaders at the said church. It was one of the traditions of the church; if one of the members sees or is in love with another, they have to tell the Pastor and pray about it.

This was quite shocking for me. For a minute, I went into complete silence and then, being all respectful, I responded, "I'm not ready for marriage, I'm only 16 years old, I don't know how to live a married life, and besides, I have to get a job". Pastor O was unhappy about my response but said "okay" and then walked away with a sorrowful face.

The thoughts of my Pastor asking that question allowed me to think about the definition of marriage. It made me introspect whether I am ready for it or not and picture myself in a relationship at a young age. I could not comprehend our conversation to the point of being afraid of facing my Pastor after that. I was not comfortable going to youth group again, knowing that one of the youth leaders had his eyes on me.

At times, when I lifted my head and looked forward, he would be staring at me. It did make me blush, but still, I had no feelings for him. It is not because he was not a fine young man; he was handsome, smart, but it was awkward for me to be in love with someone and marry that person at a tender age. However, I continued going with the purpose of having fun and partaking in the things of God.

During this time, another Christian brother from the church group approached me with his vision from God. He told me that God showed him a pretty virgin girl squeezing a boil on his face and that he should love her. The girl is in this church, and the only person he could think of was me. I responded by telling him that the devil also shows people vision and should pray about it.

CHAPTER 5:
Transportation

Transportation was exceedingly difficult to manage at times. While I was in kindergarten, we lived at a distance from the school, and I remember that I used to ride on a motorcycle to get there. Sometimes, I rode in a car in my father's absence. After moving to the fourth village, I walked to school in the mornings and came back from school for lunch. It was nearly half a mile each time. The distance did not really get to me since we walked in crowds, and during the journey, we had a good time and shared great laughs.

As I grew up and entered high school, the Bushlot Secondary, there were times when gasoline was inadequate, and that meant we had no school busses. At that time, only a few vehicles were seen out and about on the road. I used to walk approximately twelve miles from school to home in a group. This time the distance couldn't be overlooked. I remember how it used to take up all of my energy and that the moment I reached home; I was absolutely drained to do anything else. All I wanted to do was curl into the nearest place I could find and go to sleep. This was one of the reasons why I asked my dad to transfer me to the closest high school available.

That is when I got enrolled at Rossignol Secondary School, which wasn't as far as my previous school but wasn't exactly next door either. The gas shortage presented a challenge here as well. I begged rides from the sugar estate trucks that drove past the same road that I had to walk in order to reach home just so I couldn't end up exhausted at the day's end. Other times, I found ways to get on the tractor-trailers passing by. I used to run and jump on and off while it was in motion as the driver was focusing on the road. I used to get lucky on days when one of my cousins on duty drove past my school during lunch breaks. Those days I enjoyed dodging the hassle of commuting.

My dad did own a car, but it was nothing too fancy. He drove a hire car, and some of the early market vendors and school children depended upon him to catch the early morning boat crossing. I vividly remember how the car always gave him trouble when starting. There were times when we were dressed to go someplace, and the car spoiled our mood by not budging an inch. Mostly, it used to wait for the rainy days; those were the times it showed us its real face and gave us a whole lot of trouble. Every day, I used to wake up early along with my siblings to push-start the engine.

On the days when it used to pour, our front yard occasionally flooded and was filled with mud. In anticipation, I used to help my dad align coconut shells along the driveway to allow the car to have traction as we pushed the car out of the yard.

The engine of the car had a habit of shutting off exactly when it was about to reach home. My dad then used to lock its doors and walk home to get help from us, to push start the car to bring it back home. If there were passengers on the ride and were able to push, they joined us in this difficult task.

Although old, my dad kept his car clean. It was my duty to clean the car when dad and we were at home in the middle of the day for the lunch break. On other days I used to clean the car, when necessary, some mornings and evenings.

For most of my high school life, I traveled in crowded cars, with 8-10 passengers in the back seat. We used to sit on each other legs, so when we arrived at the destination, we could hardly stand as our feet would be dead and crampy.

Every day I had to walk to the Stelling Road and wait until the boat came before I could get transportation. It was usually the minibus, or if one of the car drivers recognized me and knew my parents, they would give me a ride home. Most often, the car owners were of Indian descent, and they only took the Indian student's home. If I were standing in a group, being the only black girl, they would say that they are not going as far as my destination, even though some of the same students live nearby or further than my stop.

During my nursing school life, I walked to school or to the hospital for my clinical. Yet, every now and then, I used to come across kind-hearted bus drivers or car owners who drove me to my destination free of charge, especially when it rained. At times, when I met the group to study in the evenings, one of my classmates towed me on the front bar. Sometimes, I sat on the saddle at the back. Of course, the roads were not always smooth. They had huge potholes, and numerous times when the car swerved to avoid the potholes, I would fall off in the process. But I never complained as everything was better than walking all the way home, especially on rainy nights. During my rides, I counted all the holes and mentally marked their locations. Riding during the nights was worst; not many streetlights were on the road. Although I was scared at times, I managed well. Often my nursing batch mates used to laugh at me because I never learned how to ride a bike.

CHAPTER 6:

Sick

Like every other little girl, I really enjoyed eating sweets, which caused me to have sores on my entire head and other parts of my body. These sores, when inflamed, would even ooze pus drainage. My dad had to shave my head completely at least three times to allow the sores to heal. During this time, I used to wear a white flap hat to school because I was ashamed of my buzz-cut head. I was bullied by my peers for my appearance. To care for these sores, my dad made a mixture of various herbs and bathed me three times per day, from my head to my toes, after which he applied the mixture. I was in pain and sat half-naked after these baths to allow the sores to be air-dried.

The herbs, when applied to my sores, had a very pungent and disgusting smell. It was embarrassing to go to school with these herbs on because I did not want my peers to think that I was smelly. I isolated myself as I was fearful of my peers pulling off my white flap hat, making the odor more profound. The sores oozed at times, causing the pale yellow and light pinkish puss to stain the hat. I sometimes tried to wash off these stains during the mid-day break with the hope that the only hat I owned would dry before I went back for the afternoon school session. Although not permitted in class, my teacher understood my situation and allowed me to wear my hat.

After the recurrence of the sores for the 4th time, my dad decided not to cut my hair off. Instead, he took me to see a doctor who prescribed me a pink-colored medicine. This medication was perhaps an antibiotic; however, after taking this medication, my sores were almost healed within three days. My dad also provided me with extra nourishment to ensure that my body was healing well. He also provided me enough to eat and drink, from fruits to undiluted fruit juices, which were enough to provide a decent amount of Vitamin C. I think it was a good idea, going to the doctor since his treatment actually worked. My skin did not take as much time to heal since my parents nurtured me well. I was scared of my ordeal as I thought I had leprosy, like what I had read about in the Bible.

In addition to the treatment, my dad also gave us a bitter medicine to drink during each school break. What I remember is that this "bush medicine" has a bitter yet sweet taste and was mixed with freshly squeezed coconut milk that provided a nauseating taste and scent. This concoction prepared used to be his homeopathic remedy for the neighboring kids as a "clean out. "The parents used to line their kids in our front yard awaiting this medicine. After drinking this medicine, I felt so weak from the constant vomiting and diarrhea. After taking it, we were only allowed to have water and had to drink lots of it. Due to this weak feeling, I gave the medicine the name the "through down."

CHAPTER 7:
High School Life

High school was a fun experience. I started at Bushlot Secondary and then a year later transferred to Rossignol Secondary School. While I was in 4th and 5th form, I was elected as the prefect, a position that's nowadays also known as "Head Girl." Being a leader, I had to ensure that my grades were reasonable and consistent. Likewise, I was always on time for school, easygoing, and approachable. I did track, was placed in Downer's House, which during my year was known to be the leading house in comparison to the other three houses. I was proud to be a part of the leading house and proud that I was the representative of one of the houses. I ran both 200- and 400-meters races and reached the branch level three times. I was also elected to stand by to run a relay at the highest level.

My parents did not allow me to sleep away my teenage. They always motivated and pushed us to do better and achieve all the set milestones in life. I did not have a personal trainer to train with, but that never proved to be an obstacle for me as I practiced in the village in which I lived twice every week. The other times, when I couldn't go into the village, I used our yard since it was huge. Often, I felt as though my breath had completely left my lungs, especially during the races. I suffered from stomach burns which I was told was due to my love for eating mangoes with salt and pepper, which was never advised.

I also participated in debates at school, and successfully reached the levels of inter-schools, then inter-districts, and finally inter-regions. There were times when my team won, and other times, we lost. The times we lost; I think our rebuttal pointers were not as strong. Although I did not prep enough, I tried to do my best. I also did impromptu speeches to represent my sport-house. Some of the topics were so difficult and so huge that I had no clue about them, but I tried my best.

I did not go as far as inter-school, but I did inter- houses. I also participated in drama competitions. I remember the final poem that I recited on stage was "A Treasurers' & "Monster - The Shark." This gave me second place, although I thought I would win.

I also participated during the Mashiamani season in the costume competition. One of my favorite dances was with a basket on my head, rocking colorful material clothing as I portrayed a market vendor. I danced the limbo while singing the song, *Nah eat that fish, mama, Nah eat that fish*. My group did win that competition and was sent to the city to compete against other schools. There, my group was placed second. I was not a great dancer being a Christian. I made some missteps, but they were not visible because I was in between the rows. I practiced my movements and routines at home repeatedly in front of the mirror so that my dance would be flawless. I also followed the steps religiously that were directed by our teachers.

One of my favorite subjects in school was Math. The Math teacher I had, Mr. C, drilled math into my head. His methods of teaching were impeccable and easy to understand. One of my class best friends, Spanky, also ensured that I understood the work done in school with utter clarity. He spent time after school and sometimes before school to ensure I was able to solve every difficult problem. Mr. C used to give us tests after each chapter and warned the class of posting our grades in the movie theater for all to see since most of the students used to go to the movies at least twice a week.

I also enjoyed home economics. The teachers were very compassionate and approachable. Whenever there was an event in school that involved catering, they would always invite me to be a part of a group of students to participate. Some of the things I enjoyed doing were baking sponge cake, pastries, beef or chicken patties, and cheese straw. Whenever the catering was involved in making lunch, I was overjoyed. I always made sure that I would have a big piece of chicken. I was always happy to provide my assistance since this provided the foundation in preparing me to become the cook I am today. There is where I learned how to make the best fruit punch.

CHAPTER 8:
The Death of the Love of My Life

The day my mom passed away, one of the home economics teachers took me into the home economics department and made me lie down on the bed. She comforted me and made sure that I was able to maintain a balance before I went to my class or exam. She was also very empathetic; I saw long teardrops on her cheeks, which she wiped with a tissue. She knew my mom; this was devastating to her, and for me also just the way it would be for any little girl who loses her mom at a young age.

My mom died a day before my Caribbean Excelsior examination started. Exactly two days prior to my exam, she was readmitted to the hospital due to some complications which she developed after surgery for her gallbladder. Right before my exam, she went back into the operating room to correct the medical mistake, but unfortunately, septicemia had already stepped in. Before she left our house to go to the hospital, she took off her humongous gold earrings and Timex watch and placed them into my hands. I returned her earnings, attaching them to her ears, whispering, "I want you to look pretty while you go to the doctor." I pocketed her watch since I wanted to see the time during my exam. Before she entered the car on her way back to the city to follow up with her doctor, she turned back around and gave us a good peek. I did not know that that was the last time we were seeing her alive. If I had the slightest clue, I would have given her the tightest and warmest hug.

As I went to bed the night before the exam, I just finished saying my prayers, in which I prayed for my mom and for my exam. I fell asleep only to be woken up out to the most devastating news of my life, which was, "your mom died." I received this news from one of her relatives. This was the same person who gathered a couple of neighbors and other relatives. As I got up, the house was filled with people screaming aloud. I did not believe it, but I began screaming at the top of my lungs.

From that very moment, I stopped eating, drinking, and even talking. The only thing I wanted at that time was to leave this world along with her. She was my everything. I was almost ready to give up on everything and join her. I remember clearly, one of my cousins, who is her nephew, came to pick me up from school after my first day of examination. And then he would carry and pick me up after each exam and would try to make me eat by getting me my favorite food. But I had no appetite to eat; I pushed all the food away. On the day of her burial, I could not even stand, I was so weak. I questioned God, "why my mom, why did you do this to me?" I later realized that I could not question God since he already promised me that he holds my future in the palm of his hands. They were a lot of neighbors who were comforting us; likewise, cousins and friends. My dad did not return the said day; he came two days later. It was hard for him to face us and to see our devastating state.

Losing her was traumatic for me because she was my absolute best friend. My mom is irreplaceable. Mom, you will always be in my heart forever. As I am writing this book, tears are rolling down my eyes. Whatever I have written about you is written with so much pain which I have in my heart since the day you left me. I just remember your charming smile. Although your flower may wither, or your body parts may return to dust, your charming smile, your contiguous giving spirit, and fragrance will remain in me as long as I live. I love you, but God loves you more.

After my Mother's Death, God sent me and my siblings a caring and dedicated stepmother, sister C. (You cuddle us with your warm and compassionate heart). She always believed in us and, most importantly, treated us the same way she treated her two girls. There is not even a single say where her tender loving care was different. She demonstrated incomparable love to me and my siblings. She spent a lot of time nurturing us, protecting us, guiding us and showed us what a mother's love is. I enjoyed eating the delicious dishes that she made, as those tastes still linger on my tongue.

Then at the tender age of 17, I started my nursing career just after high school. I was grateful for the opportunity when one of the tutors sent a note to one of the nurses in the village, which read, "Your application for the registered nursing program is considered." I cried until I fell out of bed. I was in disbelief as during the initial interview process, I was told that I was too young to join. I spent three years in nursing school in Guyana, in which my career was inspired after my mom's death. I was delighted as I was chosen at such a tender age to be what I always wanted to be, a nurse (this, my dreams came through).

After graduation, I was sent away to another location which is a part of the graduation process to do "outstation." I was sent to West Demerara (Best Hospital) and was assigned to oversee the pediatric unit. I did not see pediatric, simply because I cannot see children being in pain. I was too compassionate that I would cry for a kid who was suffering. I did not want to touch any of their body parts as I would inflict more pain. I was feeling the pressure to heal all their wounds immediately, so I could prevent them from suffering. It was actually very difficult for me to see them cry.

During those days, I spoiled a lot of kids by bringing and offering them candies and cookies on every shift. The kids looked forward to these treats. I also spent time reading and teaching them at their level's schoolwork, ensuring that their learning was not compromised while they were in the hospital, recovering. One of the patients wanted me to adopt her. I took care of her well and made her get back to good health. That is the reason why she decided that she wanted to live with me.

At that time, I worked evening shifts, so I had to throw my pocketbook through the window for my colleagues to catch so that I could escape the kids. As it would get dark, the kids would start crying, knowing that my shift would end soon and I would leave for home. They would whisper to me, "who will stay with us in the dark" and begin to cry.

CHAPTER 9:
Meeting with My Former Husband

One of my neighbors got married in the summer of 1985 and that is when I met my former husband. He was on a visit to Guyana and was about to leave soon. He offered me to be his girlfriend, which I accepted and became his girlfriend. Since then, this sparked a long-distance relationship. We wrote letters and sent cards for a couple of years. At times, I would not hear from him for days, but still, I held the faith and continued to think positive. I was incredibly young at that time; I would stay in the house for most of the time and would only leave if I wanted to go to church or for my duty.

Over the years, I developed that deep love for this man and continued to hold on while I was in nursing school and maintained good grades. Yes, he was my prince charming, very adorable, easy-going, and did not smoke. He would only take small drinks occasionally. He did not have many friends, and most of all, he was God-fearing. I felt confident about him just because of this one thing. Moreover, he portrayed him to be calm and collective and known to be a man of few words. That did not bother me too much since I was extremely shy.

I was extremely sad when he returned to the United States of America. After his return to America, I was told by someone that he was seeing one of my first cousins. I was able to understand that he was also corresponding to this same cousin at the said time. I felt so awkward boasting about him, but thank God, I only boasted about him to my siblings. I doubted this act at first since I did not think this man would do this to me. I felt betrayed but held on to hope. I told this to one of his cousins, who was also my cousin, my neighbor, and my best friend back then. She was the one who introduced us to each other.

Later I met his mom and siblings, in which a second sister CJ and I got extremely close. CJ used to send me money and tiny parcel whenever any of her relatives would visit Guyana. My former husband later visited Guyana for his brother's wedding, and that was the time when we both got engaged, as he asked my parents for my hand in marriage. Even on the night of our engagement, he ran off with a mixed- girl that he met at his former sister-in-law's house. It was very frustrating for me to see him being with someone else on our night of the engagement, but still, I did not give up on him. I had believed that this soon would pass, but I was left with dire embarrassment when he ran away behind another girl. Nevertheless, I did not share this with anyone; it was kept amongst my family and his family. I felt bewildered, as I did not know what to say to this man during that time. I thought that our engagement was over that very night as he told me that he was not ready for a commitment but was forced by his mother.

This was not what I was longing to hear, as I felt like disappearing in the cloud. However, I went back to work, but instead of staying over at my cousin, I travelled every day. After the fourth day, this guy began coming nearby to pick me up or would wait patiently outside his cousin's house until I got ready for date evening. I maintained my sanity then, I held on to God's promise, as he promised, never to leave me or to forsake me, nor would not make me ashamed or allow my enemies to triumph over me.

CHAPTER 10:
The Wedding

On one date night, he asked me to get married, and I being the fool, said, "yes, why not." I said to him that he is the only man I love and the one I'll get married to. The feeling of him loving me would give me butterflies and would make me feel as if I am the prettiest girl on this planet. And I always thought of him as my prince charming. He was the very first person I fell in love with, and I was ready to shower him with that love all my life.

Once everything got finalized, we started planning our wedding. I continued to walk around flashing my engagement ring with a speck of diamond even when our relationship was going through a lot of ups and downs. I never took those turbulent times of my relationship very seriously. I would just put them aside and start planning my big day. This is not because I was never bothered about those turbulences but because I trusted our relationship. I had a hope that as we will journey ourselves through life, all my wounds would have healed, and our relationship would become smoother. I would distract myself by all the wedding planning that was happening around me.

This phase of the planning was both exciting and difficult. As I was still in nursing school and it was exam period, it was quite difficult for me to give time to the wedding preparations. I would sometimes sneak out from the hospital and travel to Georgetown to make certain wedding arrangements, or at times, I would ask the sisters at the hospital for a few hours excuse. My local pastor did not want to marry us since he voiced that we are unequally yoked. Nevertheless, one of my father's friends, who was a pastor, performed the wedding ceremony.

My former mother-in-law did almost everything for the wedding since I did not have a mother. She had sent all the decoration material for the boy and girl's clothing. The cost was so little, or almost free. My wedding was very glamorous. We had 23 bridesmaids and six flower girls. His aunts wore long fancy dresses with their nicely decorated hats, and his uncles dressed in their fine-suits as they accompanied my former mother-in-law to the wedding. I was blessed enough to choose the dress which she bought.

There was a lot of food to eat and much to drink. The hall was glittering, the music with the loud beats, as his cousins danced us out to my honeymoon before midnight. But the older relatives said that I could not dance in the hall in my married dress. My honeymoon was fine, and I was so tired from the wedding ceremony. The next morning one of his aunts was gracious enough; she took us for breakfast. There she asked me, "how was your honeymoon?" which I was very embarrassed to answer.

CHAPTER 11:
Migrating to America

About a year later, I went to the United States of America to be with my former husband. Throughout the journey, I felt quite strange. I had mixed emotions. There was the happiness of being with the man I love the most and spending the rest of my life with him, but I also had a lot of fear. The ups and downs of our relationship were making me quite worried about our future. I cried halfway through my journey since I did not know what I was going to endure—being so young, in a strange land, and with none of my close siblings nearby. It was all haunting me. But then I wiped my tears and was anxious to meet my husband. I landed at John F Kennedy Airport on October 25th, 1995.

During the landing, I was amazed by all of the bright lights, so beautifully decorated. As I came out of the airplane while trying to find my way to immigration, I followed the crowd and jumped on the escalator. I did not know how to balance myself as this was new to me. I had never been on an escalator before. I went tumbling down and was very embarrassed. Some strange people came to me and offered me help. Then they grabbed my hand while I grabbed the rails. Luckily, I did not sustain any injury.

While being picked up from the airport by my former husband, I was greeted with roses and a charming smile. I felt really happy as someone was showing so much care for me. Then I stepped into a nice car, which I considered fancy then. As the journey began, my head started spinning, as I thought we were driving on roads in circles. The atmosphere had a different aroma; I was so anxious to be in the brightly lit city. I got a headache after seeing the tall skyscrapers and the humongous buildings along the highways.

This was the first time I saw so many vehicles on the road at the same time. Their lights enhanced the beauty of the atmosphere. When we got home, my mother-in-law greeted me and had also prepared dinner for me. Though I was overly excited to try the food made by her, I was feeling really full. I was also tired from the travel; all I wanted to do, was sleep. I was taken upstairs to my new bedroom, where there was little furniture, and the bed was beautifully decorated. It can be said that I was well equipped with all the things that I would need in my future life.

Surprisingly, during our married life, my former husband was also involved with someone else. Yes, he had an extramarital relationship with another Jamaican girl. When I got to know this, I was completely shattered. I could not believe the fact that the person whom I have loved so much all my life had cheated on me. But I forgave him. Since I loved him with all my heart, I could not imagine my life without him.

I never expected him to continue living that type of lifestyle after he promised to be faithful to me. Apparently, when I arrived in New York, he was trying to break off the relationship, but the girl wound never let go; she tormented and disturbed my peace for a good period of time. On various occasions, she would call me on my cell phone, but I would give it to my former mother-in-law, who lived downstairs. As she got on the phone, she began praying for this girl to leave her son and that God would find her someone else.

On a couple of occasions, it became intolerable. The calls were so annoying that I would push down one of his music sets speakers and burst some of his connecting wires while I screamed, "I will leave you. I did not enjoy being in competition, and nor am I accustomed to getting myself into fights or being a part of a warful relationship." With this entire occurrence, I did not give up. I held on to my former husband, prayed to God, and waited for things to get fixed.

CHAPTER 12:
Starting a Family

Like every other relationship, our relationship was not all gloomy and glittery. It had its ups and downs. It even went to a stage where I thought of breaking it off. But thinking about how much I loved him, I stayed in the relationship, trusting that things would work themselves out. I was holding on to the last ounce of hope - something that would give me the vision to keep going.

Love finds its way back to each other, and in our case, love conquered as well. Two years had passed, I got pregnant and gave birth to a beautiful, dark-skinned girl, the first granddaughter in his family. She was named after her two grandmothers. Our baby had bonded us more, and we got more united as a family. Everyone used to adore her so much.

Five years later, I gave birth to the second granddaughter in the family. Those little girls were a part of my heart, and I was very protective of them. We raised them remarkably; in a closely knitted family and lived in Roselle, New Jersey. We both were so proud of our daughters, especially their dad. He spent a lot of time with them, guided them, and counseled them. He took them to many amusement parks and playgrounds. He used to care for our girls while working two jobs and in school. We had this rock-solid front, and we did almost everything together. We supported each other in every possible way.

We were given the name "Batty and Pooh." Wherever we used to go, that's what we were termed as. We were the power couple. While people used to call us "Batty and Pooh," we called each other Boo and BoBo. Life was going well. Everything was working out pretty great with kids and everything. I couldn't ask for anything more. During that course, we had four homes; we purchased three, and the fourth, located in Linden, Guyana, was given to us by his parents. Although we did not have any legal documents of this gift, I used my money and did major remodeling and additions. The house looked beautiful with the state-of-the-art windows and doors. None of which were appreciated after the divorce. Instead, I was condemned by one of his parents and other family members of doing a scrappy job and making their home a mess.

Becoming a mother, I had mixed feelings. I was so excited to be called mom, yet it seemed that I didn't have any parenting skills. I didn't know a lot of things back then. Once I left my daughter with a babysitter, I felt so guilty as I had to leave her to go back to work while she was six weeks old. The only reason was that she could have a bright future. I used to work so that she could live her dreams.

At times, I would be at work, and I was just thinking about her, what she might be doing, would she be asleep or would be missing me? At that time, the technology of facetime or video calls were not available as it is today, I therefore, relied on calling the babysitter couple of times during my shift.

It was difficult for me to find a full-time job as a licensed practical nurse back then. I used to wait for the landline to ring to leave for work. Most of the time, I was there, sitting next to my landline, waiting to get a call from the nursing supervisor. I used to put myself on the on-call list at times.

I had to do this for all of the unscheduled days to ensure that I had covered forty hours for the week and worked some extra days if I did not get those hours for the following week. With this hustling, I could hardly find the time to plan for a day's event or schedule a whole day to spend quality with my beautiful girl. I wanted to play different games with her, but the work didn't let me. I used to get so tired after working a double shift. But once I was off duty, I spent quality time with her, and her father used to say, you are caring for her more than me.

I was so lucky to be living upstairs with her grandparents, and they helped me with a lot of things, and I didn't know certain things I got to know later because of them. Some days, her grandmother used to get home early from work and pick her up from the babysitter and keep her until I got home. I was relieved and stress-free when I knew she was with her grandparents or aunt since they all treated her so well and immensely cared for her. She was indeed a unique and lovable firstborn of her paternal side of the family; therefore, she was named after her grandmother.

She was calm, but she would cry aloud at night like a baby. Sometimes her grandpa would sneak upstairs, take her, and dance her to sleep while I was trying to nap for work the next day. I used a battery-operated swing to help me snoot her. My arms were so tired after holding her at night and walking the house from the front to the back and around the room. During those days, I was indeed fortunate to have supportive in-laws. Some mornings, she would wake up early and cry to be held, and they all were there for her.

We saved up some money, enough to pay down for our first home and two reliable cars. The area we planned to live in was rural and required having your own transportation since the public transport was not working out well for our work schedules. The move to Roselle, New Jersey, was smooth. We purchased our first home but did not move at the said time. Almost everything in the house was new. We decided to shift over the weekend, and I took the items I purchased in the original boxes and unpacked them. The other big items were delivered to our house either from the store or its' Warehouse. This made our move shift. All the touch-up painting I desired was completed before we moved; likewise, the closet and cupboards were neatly packed.

The place was settled, and I mostly adjusted. The next big question was, who will be watching my baby girl, while I am out on work from New Jersey to New York; while working as a nursing supervisor on double shifts. I couldn't fathom what I was exactly feeling. I was excited that I was a young homeowner and my effort to ensure my daughter was cared for. I decorated her room with crib with one of the trending Disney adventures- Winnie the Pooh bedding and matching borders and colors. As she grew a little old, I changed the color of her room to light pink and purple, which represented the princess Barbie-doll theme. I also got some of the Barbie dolls collectibles for her.

Being a stranger in a rural community, the neighbors warmly welcomed me. One of the neighbors, who lived across the street, hosted a surprise welcome party for us to meet the other neighbors. My daughter was the new baby in the town and was loved by the other children, who were much older. To the point, one of the little girl's parents offered me the entire antic of clothing and toys from her little girl. I wasn't ethical, so I was rejected. I was shy, but I also wanted to provide my firstborn with new items.

I ensured that she had the best care while I was at work; I hired the best babysitter, although I could not always afford the entire bill. During this time, her grandparents and paternal aunts helped her with the payments, which I used to feel guilty about, and sought another part-time job and ensured that she had the expenses covered.

I ensured that she was a part of all the various activities that a little girl can enjoy, from dancing in her little tutu to wearing pointe-shoes. I also ensured she had a room filled with toys to feel as happy as she could be. I also enrolled her at the Sunday children's program in church, so that she could go and talk to other kids and learn and evolve.

One day, I overheard my beautiful daughter talking alone about paying with a little girl. The conversation included teaching the person how to count and offering a reminder to complete her home assignment given by her teacher. I interrupted her conversation to find out who she was talking with, and she replied that it was her imaginary sister. I immediately knew that she was lonely, and she was asking in her ways for a sibling. That was when I decided that we needed to plan for another kid.

It quickly happened, but unfortunately, I had a miscarriage. I was astonished and scared of being a failure as I did not know how to break this news to her as she was thrilled and doing her best to protect the little one in her ways. I was extremely sad for days; tears were continuously falling off my eyes; more so, I had the dead fetus in me waiting for my doctor's availability to perform the dilatation and curettage.

This was driving me crazy until I shared it with my former brother-in-law, who knew someone from the hospital, and he told me to get it done with immediately to avoid harm. Due to him, I underwent the procedure in a timely fashion.

A few months later, I was pregnant with another baby. I was more careful this time than the last time. Two months into the pregnancy, my father died as time went by, and I traveled to bury him... As the delivery date grew closer, I did not know the sex of the baby as I wanted it to be a surprise.

My former in-laws played the guessing and betting game, and her grandpa won the bet. I had three different baby showers between my two jobs and on various shifts. Therefore, I did not have a family baby shower since I had many gifts. The next thing was giving birth to another beautiful girl. At last, my older daughter now had the imaginary sister she was longing for. I was comfortable with having two girls and was not planning on having more children. I begged my doctor for a tubal ligation, but he refused, stating that I was too young and may change my mind later.

But I was persistent, there were many times I pleaded with him, but he was constantly ignoring me. It was just before Christmas; I planned and called his office, and I was like, this would be the last time I would ask him, and he agreed. Before I knew it, we planned the procedure. I was delighted and was looking forward to this appointment so that my fears of becoming pregnant again and enduring those dreadful feelings would be over.

During the pre-procedure work-up, I got a call from the doctor stating that my Beta count was high and I was pregnant, but it could be a miscarriage. I got worried and told him that he might have the wrong patient. He confirmed that he had called the right patient and asked me to state my birthday. He read the laboratory report and instructed me to go immediately to the emergency room at Saint Barnabas Hospital.

I was in disbelief that this was happening to me. I immediately stepped off the ladder and concluded my Christmas cleaning and decorating. I told my 5-year-old daughter that I was delighted to have finished decorating the house, greeted her, and left her and her sister with her grandparents.

While I was in the emergency room, I had a sonogram which confirmed that I had an ectopic pregnancy, and it was at the tip of the tube. I got a pre-procedural work-up and was then sent to the operating room for a tubal ligating. My husband took them to the hospital to see their mother.

It was frightening to my 5-year-old daughter, who accompanied me with her baby sister in the car seat, who was just four months old. My older daughter turned to me and asked if I would die, and I said no, but whispered to her that I was getting another baby, but it was stocked into my tube; it would not survive, so the doctor must remove it.

She looked at me with her round-little face and bright eyes as she said, "mom Melanie is a little baby, and you are having another baby." I did not respond to her, as I was out of words. The doctor detoured from doing the tubal ligation at this point, stating that I had only one tube and, yes, I was pregnant.

Raising two beautiful girls was heart-rending, and they kept each other company closely. They were well behaved. Unlike my older daughter Mary, Melanie was quieter as a baby. She was not a crier. You never knew that a baby was in the house until you visited. I sometimes wonder if she had a voice. I tried so hard so that she would cry or at least say something.

They both attended private school and were engaged in piano, dance, and various sports and clubs. Additionally, swimming lessons and learning a second language were also part of their schedule. It was fun attending their dance recital and games, though, at times, I might just catch the ending part or miss the entire session. They knew that I was either at work or school if I did not show up. I used to feel guilty when I could not attend the games or concerts that they were performing.

They both grew gracefully. Time had gone by swiftly. The older was in high school, and I was planning for her sweet sixteen. I thought she was so quiet that she did not have friends, not until she gave me the list of children, she wanted to invite to her birthday party. She said everyone on the list must be invited. In total, there were 144 children.

Together with her paternal side of her family, we managed and gave her a sweet sixteen, which will be her lifetime memory. As her friends from Roselle catholic stated, that was the birthday party for a decade. She looked beautiful, and everyone said that I did a fabulous job. I almost got into trouble since more than half of her friends who attended her school did not show up for classes the next day.

I realized that Mary was getting older when she told me that she got an invitation from a guy to take her to prom, and it was so special, as it was placed on a piece of pizza. We went shopping to get her a dress for the prom from a boutique with hot prices, and I got her a beautiful gown that was altered to fit her. Then we decided that she should go to the salon for her hair followed by her make-up at home.

I dressed her to the point that people often wait to see what she will show off in. They gathered along my path this time as they welcomed her out of our home and into the limousine, then off to the park to take her pictures. I did not accompany her for the picture taking since she would feel shy among her peers; I asked one of her friends who had already graduated to take her picture per my daughter's request. Of course, she looked stunning, and I could not imagine my firstborn all grown-up and looking this gorgeous. My heart was melting.

She excelled academically, as she was placed on the school's honor roll. She developed a love for math; when she was a little girl, I had her enrolled in the KUMON program. She did not like it, and after a while, she hid some of the booklets. Not until I received calls from the KUMON center that some of her booklets were missing that I immediately searched and discovered those booklets stuffed in her pillow and some underneath her mattress. I realized that she had enough, and she hated the repetitious math. And then, I had a long conversation with her that we would soon end the program since Math was already on her fingertips.

It was soon the time for college applications. I was not provided much guidance during the application process; she depended on her guidance counselor, who did not administer the process smoothly. Nevertheless, she was accepted into a few expensive colleges, even with scholarships. Others, she was placed on their waiting list. Those colleges were not that expensive and were pretty affordable.

She was selected in several colleges, so choosing one was an arduous task for her. Still, she decided and made up her mind that she would be getting enrolled in Jersey City University. As it was closer to home, I was happy, and I could pop in to drop off food and anything that she needed. And even, it was pretty affordable.

I was doing well until she made a college move-in list and gave it to me. I paused for a while and did a reality check. I was in disbelief that she was moving out and living on campus. I did not think she was ready for this since she was raised too sheltered, to the point when I sent her to dump the garbage to the curbside, she would ask me to look at her through the window. I was questioning myself, should I let her stay on campus or commute daily? These thoughts lingered with me for a couple of weeks until I looked at the safety elements and realized how dangerous it would be for her to drive amongst the huge trucks along her route to school, and I decided that she should live in a dorm.

It was time for move-in; I drove her there along with my younger daughter and sister; I cried as I unpacked her stuff. I tried to hold back my tears and stayed vital for my little one, who was so attached to her. My inner being was torn apart; I wiped my tears and started praying, asking God for his protection and safety, and granting her the knowledge to make the right choices and decisions and not linger into temptations.

I had long conversations with her about living on campus. My colleagues at work and some of the nursing students I encountered shared this information with me. However, I just left her at the mercy of God, hoping that she would follow my rules. Nevertheless, I know that she had to walk on this journey towards life to accomplish her dreams. My fear was, what if she would be in a room by herself and something happened to her? What was the timeframe before someone will know? I was just worried about the timely room check.

Therefore, one of the rules was daily calls to check-in, and she must call me every time she was leaving the campus. I used to stay up late until I knew she was back in her room safely. When she had her late classes, she must call me when she was leaving to go back to her dorm. She ensured that my heart was at ease by following the rules. I sometimes threw a text in, hoping that she would respond, even though no phones should be on during her class. I would get that immediate response; she followed the rules well. I was also fearful of all the on-campus parties, as students would often consume alcohol and use drugs; that was my biggest nightmare, but I hope that she was not pressured into doing so.

Then I think about sororities and their initiation. I was just thinking through some of their processes, and they seemed scary; I hope that her roommate or other friends would not convince and pressure her to join. Not so much of being apart, I fear the worst during the initial phase as she may not cope with all of their requirements. I did not want to hear any negative comments about this group and my daughter's enduring. The imagination of the initial phase brought tears to my eyes and gave me goosebumps. I did mention this to her, and she reassured me that she would not join anything like that and I should not waste my time thinking about something that would not occur.

The news of having her having a boyfriend gave me a headache, although I knew this was next. When the hormones are at their peak, children want to feel for love and belongings. She first introduces this fine young man as a friend. He was humble, warm-hearted, and mannerly from the moment I met him. I then became the investigator asking questions about his dorm. Firstly, I wondered about his accommodation on campus by finding out if they shared the same building. Oh my God, when he said that they shared the same building, but on a different floor, I was speechless.

I had a lot in my head. I thought, what if they were having sex, but I did not want to ask it or do anything to scare him away. I mumbled on that question that I do not believe they both heard it or if they both ignored me. I immediately switched the question to learn more about his major, grades, and family background. I also asked them if their relationship was serious; they answered yes. I internalized and could hardly digest that my daughter was in love. The young man visited during family events, and I welcomed him with open arms.

Like most parents, I got straight to the point on the topic of having sexual intercourse with my daughter. I knew that my daughter would not discuss this. I then began to talk about teenage pregnancy and its implications. I went into sexually transmitted diseases and pregnancy and their impact on life. I also reiterate the importance of completing college and getting a permanent job.

She then switched her major; we then began a conversation about the importance of higher education to work in her capacity. During her years living on campus, she shared many stories about her roommates; I constantly encouraged her to come home during the weekends. At times, I feel like the lawyer, always trying to instigate everything.

I seldomly visit, but I cook multiple dishes for her to take back and or drop-offs. I was also juggling two jobs and completed my doctorate at the said time. We spent much time on the phone, and I would plan trips and vacations around when she was free. She often voiced the feeling of being left out from family events. She sometimes verbalized how she could not wait to finish college to be home and go out and have fun. I will remind her that there is a time for everything. You must be patient and focus on your goals as she would use the term. I admire your perseverance and wish I could be like you one day.

My second girl, Melanie, was the opposite child. She's more fashionable and outgoing. She cares and loves humanity and, of course, is a social butterfly. As a tinning cup knocks, she must be present. She was the leader of her pack and always got into trouble.

I hid from her teachers, as I was tired of hearing complaints about her talking a lot. When she could not do it in the classroom, she took her classmates to the bathroom to talk. At times she overspends her time in the bathroom, causing her teachers to go and find her. The days I do lunch duties at her school, she can hardly wait to go on break just to run her mouth, and at times, she takes the lead role.

During her pre-school days, the students stood up and cheered her as she walked into her seat. She was a lover of most of her teachers, and she would draw on the chalkboard the teachers' smiley faces. If they were at a party or when she did not have to wear her school uniform, she picked the most fashionable outfit and pre-plan her appearance in Infront of the mirror. Additionally, they assumed the students' gestures and showed off their costumes. While attending Shim's academy, she can hardly wait for her birthday party in school, so the principal will announce her name as he wishes her happy birthday through the intercom.

She was involved in many activities, from dancing to sports, and it was exceedingly difficult for me to take her to all the events while working. At times I showed up for the first or the last part of her games to cheer and encourage her. She loves music as she plays the piano and sings in her school choir. She had a hard time changing school when I moved from New Jersey to New York as she feared losing her friends and going to a new school, the students would not like her. On the second day of her new school, she was already in a chosen girl's group, and upon seeing how she interacted and socialized, it was as if she knew them from her childhood. I was blustered.

At times, you cannot take these kids. She made me feel guilty as if I had moved and made her change school on purpose. It got to the point that I even cried in front of the principal, who reassured me about giving her one week, and I would not believe what I saw. Moreover, after her first day at school, she told me that she was the only afro-American in her class and as she walked in, the entire class stared at her. I reassured her that you are new, and anyone who hears of a new student is curious to know more about the person and meet them.

One of the girls' groups that she was in had a home down the shore, and they all had a routine of going together. I was hesitant to send Melanie since I did not know the girl's parents that well. My daughter insisted and arranged for the meeting of these parents ahead of time and had us exchange telephone numbers. I do not approve of sleepovers, much more go-away trips. I breached my rules to get her to "fit in," as she called it. I felt comforted since one of my friend's parents is a police officer and a school teacher.

I packed her bag, and she went and had fun with the girls. She checked in twice a day, and I reiterated my dos and don'ts while reminding her that I did not consult her father. By this time, I felt that I was raising her by myself since she forced me to change her school since she was not assisting in her transport. She sent pictures of the group at seaside height, even riding on the beach.

Melanie had many friends; I always had to cater to a massive group at her parties. Even though she told me that only a few friends would be coming, a later big crowd showed up. She said that about twenty of her friends would be coming; the entire backyard was filled with her friends. During the lockdown for COVID-19, we kept her birthday party with the limitation of six friends coming. Nevertheless, these six came at intervals totaling eighteen to twenty-four. She had two hundred guests at her glamorous sweet sixteen parties, of which forty were family and my friends. The remaining were her friends.

I decided that Melanie needed to be more mature and responsible until I held back her permit to drive at sixteen. I can hardly live the nightmare of her going while looking and fixing her make-up, her re-attaching her eyelashes while she was driving, and missing the emergency vehicles. I can hardly imagine how she would be blasting her music loudly, missing her turn or direction. As she approaches eighteen, I felt she is more mature and will adhere to safety while driving. She finally got her permit; I was nervous as she stepped into the driving school. I uttered, may God have his way and protect all the other drivers, likewise, her.

Melanie is preparing for college in two months, and I cannot wait. She has expensive taste, is very glamorous, and is high maintenance. Additionally, I love costly vacations and staying while posing at the camera to keep the memories. Oh, I can hardly wait to see her succeed along her career path to represent and support herself. We often joked about her being rich to stand her expensive taste. She has a part-time job and gets the pay every other Friday, by the said Saturday, she is asking me for some money. She loves to spend and would give inexpensive gifts; she has a heart for the beggars on the street and the less fortunate; she thinks of them constantly and prefers to provide them with her last dollar. You must love this girl.

My first son was life-changing; this occurred when I was more mature and almost completed my career path. I did not have to worry about the hassling and bustling of building life. I was more stable and felt more ready to be a mother. I am not sure if this was because of the boy or the feelings of being prepared. Ben brought much joy and happiness to my life. He's so cute and bright, gives hugs and kisses. In addition, he is funny and very active. He often gets you on your toes and keeps your eyes busy in search of his next move.

With Ben, you must plan one week as he's growing; he loves technology and figures out how to use it without knowing anything. He forced me to childproof my house to ensure he was safe. Although the cupboards have locks, he sticks a butter knife or fork to open the doors. We placed safety gates to prevent him from climbing the stairs, but they were of no use; he discovered how to open and close them. He learned how to put the television on and get his favorite shows. I must sleep with one eye open to ensure that I am aware of his whereabouts.

Ben is attached to the girls and often cries to sleep and hang out late with them. They let him have his way and often bring back treats for him when they go out. He would search their rooms for candy and pocketbooks for gums, and he touched their personal items in their room during that search. With Ben, you much lock your room. Often, he makes his mischiefs, then comes back with a conning face and a soft voice whispering, "I'm sorry, I would not do that again." His personality wins your heart.

Having my second son Seth, was hard at the beginning for Ben, as he thinks that Seth is stealing his limelight. He took away all his toys from him and took the greatest advantage at first. Seth being noticeably quiet and humble then, would give everything up and stay quiet until he gained enough strength and size to defend him. Although Ben would not share anything with Seth, Seth would often look for him and ensure he gave him part of what he had.

Not until Seth realized that even his toys were being taken away, did he began fighting back. He scrambled Ben and bit him to prove his point. Seth is now aggressive and does everything that his brother did. He can talk and verbalize his needs; he spoke clear and operated any technology since he was one plus. He knew how to get to whichever YouTube program he chose and clear any pop-up messages or advertisements. He loves to climb and reach whatever he wants. Overall, my last row is caring and loving; he often expresses his gratitude to all at home. I usually smile as he says, "mommy, I love you," and I ask him how much, and he always says, "thirty."

As I moved to New York, I briefly had the entire time at home with kids. The school was on lockdown due to COVID-19, and Melanie chose to continue high school from home; seeing that the students are not following the set COVID-19 guidelines; she feels safer at home. The little kids would hang out with the older and have fun. At times, it is too noisy in the house. The little crying as they cannot get their way while the older playing music aloud. When it comes to eating, the older like spicy food, and the younger try the same, but later come crying because their mouths are on fire.

The little boys were more attached to Melanie as Mary spent most of her younger days in college. To see them interacting with boys is amazing. Now the boys often ask, "Is Mary and Melanie home" or, "I want to go to Mary and Melanie." I am already preparing them for the move, as we will be moving to Florida, and Mary will not be coming, while Melanie will be going off to college. I hope with this move and the boys starting school there, they will find their peers to play with to have a wonderful scheduled life and a routine. [cont.]

Whenever you are moving to a new place, there is a different kind of excitement. You are happy and yet so nervous at the same time. That's exactly what was happening to me. I had an assortment of emotions about this move; I hated the separation of my kids, they all love each other so much, but due to being far, they were not connected with each other that well. I had seen all of my kids craving that unity, that bond as a family.

Whenever they all would be together on holidays, it would be a totally different level of excitement and happiness. All of the kids used to have so much fun, my daughters would indulge my little boys in different activities. In short, we had a blast together. But, once the vacations were over, it wasn't the same. The boys were missing their sisters, and the sisters would call me and tell me how much they were missing the house.

That is why I wanted to move so that we can all be together under the same roof. It would help my kids to grow closer to each other. Plus, we would be going to move to a warmer climate; in an area where the boys could play freely and feel inclusive. The environment is harmless and sociable there; the kids can walk to the playground without worrying about anything. I do love the fact that the community is surrounded by sidewalks and a park in which we can walk anytime, as it is open 24 hours. I was so ready and looking forward to this move.

I cannot wait to say Goodbye to New York, and scream, "here I come, Florida!!"

CHAPTER 13:
Losses

Losing My Best Friend

Losing someone is the most painful thing. Your whole body aches. It is hard to conclude the pain that one goes through after losing someone close. When a person is going through such a loss, he or she goes through a lot of emotions. Losing someone can be hard to recover from.

We understand death only after it has placed its hands on someone we love. ***-Anne L. de Stael***

The first tragedy that I ever faced was losing my best friend ML. Since the moment I understood what friendship exactly was, ML had been my friend. She was like a sister to me—a person who had helped me a lot in my life. I can't explain in words what she meant to me. I was always very thankful and grateful to have her in my life. She was the most genuine person that I ever met, and she had proved it through her friendship as well.

One day, I got a message from her mother that she was in the hospital. She said ML wasn't going to make it and that her situation was really critical. I couldn't digest that information; I just couldn't accept it. I was in a state of shock, yet the tears didn't stop. I asked for the hospital details from her mother, but that hospital was very far.

I was too young to travel by myself; hence I was waiting for my dad to come back home and take me to visit her, not knowing that she was left with lesser time than I expected. When I reached the hospital, she was already dead. I felt so devastated. I started regretting why I couldn't come early. I wasn't even able to say goodbye to her. I cried so much, questioning why did she leave me like that. She didn't give me a chance to talk to her in her last moments. I was so alone, not having anyone around. She was my best friend, and it was such a tragic loss.

When I was a kid, I believed only old people die. After her death, my whole belief system changed, and I had a clearer understanding that irrespective of age, anyone can die. I had a hard time coping with her death and grieved so much. Even today, I still remember her charming smile, her long pretty braids of her fluffy hair, and her dance moves. She was always dancing around me, showing me her cutest moves. ML, you will always be in my heart.

Losing My Mother

One of the greatest nightmares anyone can face is losing their mother at a tender age. I was 16 years old when my mother died, and I can never erase that memory from my head. It was the worst day of my life.

My high school exams were starting, and I was preparing for them. It was the night before my first exam when my mother died. Although it seemed unreal, I found it difficult to face the reality of losing her. Her death left me numb. I was feeling lost, insensitive, miserable, enraged, frustrated, and disturbed.

My mother was my best friend; we used to share everything. She stood like a rock on my toughest days. She played an important role in my life, especially when I would not study for any exam. Whenever I had to study for a test or exam, she would prepare snacks. She didn't only just make snacks for me, but at times she also got up from her sleep to make sure she kept me company, even if it costs her having few hours before going to work. Sometimes, she would fall asleep in the chair while waiting for me to complete my study.

The moment I got the news of her death, it did not sit well with me; I froze for a while, and I got blank. Then I started screaming at the top of my lungs; I do not think that there were enough barrels to catch my tears. Everything was changed, nothing was the same without her.

I had lost a vast amount of weight; refused to eat or drink for about three months. For days, I had a bitter taste in my mouth and that weird feeling of fullness. I loved her so much, and with every passing breath, I was missing her more and more. When I would be in the house by myself, I used to miss her presence and the way she used to rub her hands around my hair and pat on my shoulders every now and then.

There was a different kind of fear that had grown inside of me. I was always scared around the house, even though there were people in the house, I would be fearful of going upstairs. Sometimes, I think I saw her shadow flashes across the room; as I tried to take a clearer peak, the shadow disappeared.

I don't know if those were my imaginations or it was all happening in real. But you know what was real, my love for her. Years had passed, and I still miss her.

Losing My Father

A father is an idol for daughters. He is like a shade on a sunny day, an umbrella in the rain. Even the thought of losing a father is scary. It shakes your soul.

I dreaded the day my dad departed. He died while I was pursuing my bachelor's degree. He lived with me for a couple of years in Roselle, New Jersey. I still reminisce some of the good old days we used to spend together. At times, when I cooked dinner, he would simply say, "Do not eat as yet, lay the table and wait until I come back." He quickly jumped into his little blue car, stating, "I am going up the road and come back." The next thing I noticed on his return, were two brown paper bags in his hands with grease on the outside.

The high fragrance of Chinese food stimulated my salivary glands. He then put it out on the table and stated, "Dinner is being served, put up your food for next day, and let us eat something different."

My father was a well-groomed security officer who worked at Rahway hospital before he resigned and went back to Guyana to live his life. He was really sad the day he told me he resigned from his job because he had made up his mind that he would be going back to Guyana to live.

I was astonished at first, but later I said to him, if this is what will make you happy, then I need you to be happy as well. I had taken out a life insurance policy for him, he also canceled it since he would not be living in the US any longer.

Before his departure, he went to the store and ensured he bought me a tiny electrical aquarium with fish and said that I should keep it always. I loved that aquarium. I used to watch those tiny fishes, swimming in that little aquarium, and I still have it.

While he was leaving my house, I got very upset and I cried a lot. Not only was he great company at home, but he was also a huge help for us. Whenever we would be watching a movie, he would never stop doing his commentary—suggesting alternative endings.

Once, we watched the Titanic movie together, and I saw him crying while watching it. He cried his eyes out. I never knew my dad had these many emotions.

One early morning, after I finished drinking my hot, black tea, my phone rang. It was my dad calling to see how I was feeling after he found out that I was having my second child, but I was extremely sick. He then said he would come back to take care of me. He asked me to book him tickets, so he could catch a flight and come see me.

I was so excited that he was coming back! I couldn't help but think that we could continue enjoying the good time we'd shared.

Two days later, I got another telephone call. I thought it was from my dad, and he wanted to ask if I wanted anything? But it was my younger brother, and he asked if I had heard about daddy? I said yes, he's coming back to America to take care of me. He said no, he just had a stroke, and we took him to the hospital.

Everything just got paused, I didn't know how I was supposed to react. I was excited for him to be back, and now I was hearing this. I was so shattered.

But he pulled through and was later transferred to my brother's house in New Amsterdam Berbice to be close to a rehabilitation center. During this time, one of my friends and batch-mates, who is a medic, was checking on him almost daily. My father was recovering very fast, which even gave me strength. He was able to walk with support after sustaining some residual weakness. He was improving.

My younger brother was always there looking after him. One afternoon, he told him that he was going to take a bath, then he will put him to bed. My dad got agitated and said no, just rub my feet first. While my brother was rubbing his feet, he noticed that he was sweating profusely.

Worried, my brother started shouting, "Dad?? Are you okay?? Dad?" But there was no answer. He later heard loud snoring as though he had gone into a deep sleep. My brother tried to wake him up, but there was no response. Hence, he rushed him to the hospital; perhaps on their way to the hospital, he died. Receiving this news was devastating; I was screaming on top of my lungs and was in a state of denial. I even hit the wall so hard. I was endlessly crying while screaming "DAAAADDD."

All the memories of the good times will stay with me, and I will cherish them always. All the laughter, fun, movie sessions, unaccounted surprises, and everything little thing he did for me. Each and every detail linked to him will always live with me.

I had to travel to Guyana to bury him. During this time, I was pregnant with my second daughter and was suffering from severe hyperemesis gravidarum ,which I was treating with 'Tigan' (anti-nauseated medication) through a subcutaneous pump. Every food that I consumed while in America, I couldn't digest it and ended up throwing up. I could not even swallow my own saliva; I was in such a bad condition.

I reached Guyana, all devasted. We all were burying my dad. It was the saddest day of my life, and my tears weren't stopping. He might have been gone but would never be forgotten. I love you, Dad!

Losing My Brother

A brother and sister's relationship are unmatchable. They are like tom and jerry, but in need, they are there for each other. The bond that siblings share is undoubtedly the best in the world. No matter how tough the situation gets, a brother will always be there to support his sister, and the sister would be there to hug her brother on his lows.

Imagine the pain of losing a brother; it is as if a piece of you is snatched from you - so harshly that you are scarred for life. The same thing happened to me as I got the news of one of my older brother's death; I was in a state of shock. I knew my brother was not doing well; doctors had said that the chances of surviving were less. But still, receiving that shocking news on that evening caught me by surprise the same way as my parents.

I was at work, my phone kept ringing, but I ignored it as I had to submit an urgent project. After getting free, I took my phone out of my bag, and there were multiple missed calls from various members of my family. I really did not think it was that serious. After a tiring day at work, I glanced at my phone and realized the unusual missed calls as I got into my car. I started thinking what it could be about but was scared to return the calls. I even received a message marked as urgent from my mother's friend. I got so scared, thinking about what it could be about, and finally decided to call back.

I dialed my mother's friend, and she picked up the call and said, "Did you hear what happened?" she took a pause, "I have been trying to get you since this morning."

My heart was racing, and I was getting a very heart-sinking feeling. I quickly asked, "Is everything okay?" and I even attempted to answer my question, "Do not say no, please."

She was, of course, silent and tried to whisper. The words could not get out of her mouth. I was nervous and immediately began having gripes in my abdomen. My hand felt so weak and was sweating, and I started trembling; she then said that your brother passed away this morning.

Before she could utter these words (your brother), I began screaming very loudly. "Aaaaa, nooo!! It cannot be true; tell me you are lying." She said, "No, it's true."

I gathered myself and replied, "Okay, I am coming."

I started feeling cold all of a sudden. I was so numb, and every inch of my body was shaking. And even I was feeling so heavy-hearted in the morning, and now this had happened. I cried through the way from the office to my parents' house.

I reached and searched for my brother. His body lay still in his coffin, so peacefully and relaxed. His head was a little crooked, but one of my sisters placed her hand and straightened it. He looked so refreshed laying there, his soul at rest. My brother was the kindest person I ever knew, and he will always be there with me.

I will miss him greatly for his laughter, warmth, and positivity. His sense of humor was one of the most elite I knew of, accompanied by a very giving heart. He packed us with kiddie's treats during his trading era. I will continue to cherish the good memories that we shared. I curled and reached his ear and said, "Sleep on in paradise, my dear brother Kempton. You will never be forgotten!

CHAPTER 14:
Grief

"Grief is the most peculiar thing; we are so helpless in the face of it. It's like a window that will simply open of its own accord. The room grows cold, and we can do nothing but shiver. But it opens a little less each time, and a little less, and one day we wonder what has become of it." **-Arthur Golden**

Grief had become a regular part of my life. I kept losing people, and the cycle was going on and on in a continuous loop. I couldn't recover from one traumatic loss, and immediately there was another one waiting for me.

My Other Brother

This book would not have been completed without my brother being a part of it. I was hesitant and had no strength to share this part of my life. I would have been guilty if this integral part of his story had been kept from the readers, and they wouldn't know how much he loved humanity and his impact on people's lives. My brother, who could have gotten to the extreme to help their loved ones, would be there to support me in the blink of an eye. I could not afford to dismiss how his death affected me and impacted the entire family.

I had to gain a lot of strength, align my thoughts, and put them into perspective before proceeding. I felt I would not be true to myself and him if I minus his story. So, I wanted to mention his story as a tribute to my handsome and God-fearing brother. He was so close to me, and losing him was as if I had lost a part of myself. It was so hard to deal with it; hence I wanted the world to know how I coped with his death.

Sundays were meant to be chill and fun, where a family would do chores together or watch a movie with each other, but not this one. It was the 28th of February, 2021, and I just finished cooking chicken chow Mein and ate a small bowl of it. I took the dishes to the sink and started cleaning them. I had my hands dipped in the water when the phone rang.

I was expecting a call from my younger sister is Guyana, so I was not surprised. She was supposed to call me to discuss one of her in-law's burial arrangements who had just lost the battle of his life three hours ago. Even she called me a while back and cried on top of her lungs; I asked what happened? Then she told me about the sudden death of her uncle-in-law. I was consoling her, but she was sobbing uncontrollably. I felt so bad for her and tried to help her out until our call was interrupted as someone asked her to help her with something. She said that she would call me later. So, I thought it would be her.

I dried my hands and answered the phone; it was indeed my sister from Guyana calling back as expected, but the call was not for the burial arrangements of her in-laws; it was something utterly devastating. The phone was pressed against my right ear, and all I was hearing were screams. I thought she was despondent because of the death, and then she started saying something in a shouting kind of way, which I could not understand at all. I only understood one word, and that was death.

I asked her to repeat herself in a slow tone to understand her. She paused, took a deep breath; her breath was shaky, and then she stated, "I don't know how to say it, but we have a death at our house." I was flummoxed and said, "Yeah, I know one of your uncles-in-law died?"

She sighed so loud that I could even sense her pain and then said, "Our brother is no more with us."

I couldn't think of anything and hung up the call, thinking it might not be true. I was in disbelief and started screaming so loud. I still was not believing in it until I got calls from several other family members.

I was still in dismay, and my heart was aching so hard while my screams echoed the place. I was still in despair and wanted to confirm it; I shook up while thinking whom to call. I thought of calling someone who lived close by him, so I dialed my nephew's number, and he picked it up.

I asked him if the news circulating was true, he replied, "Yeah, unfortunately, he couldn't make it." I disconnected the call and started walking here and there in a circular motion; I was shocked and shaken to the core.

During this time, my husband was upstairs preparing to go to work; he was scared for me and did not know how to console me during that hard time. He questioned whether he should go to work and if I would be, okay? I just nodded while crying. I had my two little boys with me, and my girls were at work. I did not want to disturb their workflow, so I didn't call them and waited until they got home. My twenty-two-month-old son sprayed my hair while his older brother (three years old) combed my hair and wiped my tears while kissing me. They tried their best to reassure me in their ways.

I still was in disbelief, so I asked for a picture to confirm my brother's death. Moments later, I received pictures of him lying dead; his body was gruesomely destroyed such that it was beyond recognition, his skull lay open, face scarred with multiple lacerations, and his extremities with multiple compound fractures.

Surprisingly, not much bleeding. But my brother's motorcycle was in pieces, and personal belongings were scattered. One thing for sure, one of his hands was lifted above his head with his eyes open. … I can only imagine as he says goodbye world, his hand was raised to heaven saying to God, here I am master, I'm ready for your kingdom.

I started feeling cold all of a sudden. I was so numb, and every inch of my body was shaking. And even I was feeling so heavy-hearted in the morning, and now this had happened.

My brother always preached, and he always says that God does not care about our bodies but our soul. He always lets us know that no one knows - the time or the hour of our death, but we must always be prepared.

He told us this one thing a lot: "To be absent in the body is to be present with the lord." He was a powerful man of God, a pastor, a husband, a bother, an uncle, a brother-in-law, an uncle-in-law, a son-in-law, a cousin, and a friend of many.

My brother was the kindest person I ever knew, and he will always be there with me; I will miss him a lot for his laughter, warmth, and positivity. His sense of humor was one of the most elite I knew, accompanied by a very giving heart. He packed us with kiddie's treats during his trading era. I curled and reached his ear and said, "Sleep on in paradise, my dear brother. I will never forget you!"

After coming from his burial, I browsed my phone to see some of our shared messages. T

he last text he sent on 1/1/2021 (New Year's Day) @17:23 "Thanks be unto Almighty God who brought us into 2021. While there is great uncertainty about our future, let's be reminded that God holds and knows our future. Therefore, let us place our lives into his hands, for he has good plans for us."

I scrolled a bit up, there was another text, "We have moved closer to the end of time; our lives need to be in the state of readiness for Jesus is returning a day and hour that we don't know.

Let us practice righteousness, obey the gospel, and remain faithful to the end. As you the lord, I declare that the blessings of God that make you rich and no sorrow would be all yours through the end of this year. God bless you and your family."

I also saved all the pictures he posted on Facebook on my phone.

Oh, how I miss my brother. RIP Pastor McKenley Farley.

Gone too soon, I love you and would remember you always as being:

O- Outstanding

K- Kindhearted

E- Enthusiastic

C- Caring

H- Helpful

I- Independent

F- Faithful

A- Attentive

R- Reliable

L- Loyal

E- Entertaining

Y- Youthful

My dearest brother, although your flower may wither, your fragrance remains; I love you, but God loves you more. God needed more angels like you; continue to sleep in eternal peace until we meet again.

My Father-in-Law

The massive outbreak caused by the coronavirus has wrapped the whole world in its spell. Everything was severely affected due to the COVID-19, be it the social aspect or economic. And it is not just the social and economic aspect that is at stake, human lives are equally at risk. Thousands of people were dying each day due to this deadly virus, and that's precisely how I lost my father-in-law. On March 3rd, I answered a call from my father-in-law's practitioner while I was at my job teaching. Usually, he would not call that early, it was the first time, and I assumed it was serious. Initially, I was hesitant to answer the phone because I knew he wasn't doing well, and hearing about his pain made me want to visit him, but due to COVID-19, I couldn't.

Finally, I picked up the call and talked to the practitioner. He told me about my father-in-law's condition and said he was not doing well. He said coronavirus was failing his organs; it started affecting his lungs; both lungs stopped functioning and were spreading towards the kidneys. He was already provided artificial oxygen, and now looking at the current situation, we might have to move him to vent. I couldn't fathom that information, and drops of tears fell off my eye. I was out of words, I had no idea what to say to him, and I just stayed blank for about a minute until I finally spoke with a cracked voice, "So, is he going to be okay?"

He said, "Well, Ummm. We can't promise anything; we are trying our best, but the chances are less." He continued, "Tell your husband that too; now I gotta go, my staff is calling." And then he disconnected the call.

After that, I was standing in the same position, thinking about my father-in-law's affectionate smile and how he used to treat me like her own daughter. It made me sad, I knew he was suffering, but this was just too much. Thinking about it made me feel powerless; I couldn't do anything for him except pray and hope for his recovery.

I was thinking about my husband at that moment and how he would feel and react to this. I couldn't focus on the class, so I decided to go home early. I asked my students to complete their due assignment for the following week, and I released a case study based on my father-in-law's condition and advised the students to formulate a plan of care to see how they would handle the situation. I wanted to ensure that they could care for the patient and family when they faced a problem. I quickly drafted the case study that told my students to plan for this case as their homework with tears in my eye.

I got out of the class and left for the house. The purpose of leaving work early was to go home and support my husband in this challenging time. I knew he wouldn't take it well, and it would be difficult to absorb all of that; that's why I needed to be there with him.

My husband was surprised to see me this early, and he sensed something was wrong. I told him that I got a doctor's call and his dad wasn't doing well. They would move him to vent, but the covid is causing total organ failure. My husband got zoned out, he loved both of his parents more than anything in the world, and he wasn't able to meet them for ten days because they were in isolation; it was already killing him. Now when I said all of that, he was crushed inside. I went and hugged him and said, don't worry, just pray.

After a day, we knew that his condition had worsened, and we all were devastated to hear it. His situation wasn't getting any better; instead, it kept getting more critical. As we were uncertain about the next day and his survival chances were slim to none, I asked my husband to visit his dad. But due to the whole covid situation, the hospital was not permitting any visitation. My husband wanted to see his father, and he asked me to do something. Being a nurse, I tried talking to the doctor. I told him that I respect the hospital rules, but you should look at the situation's sensitivity here and alter them slightly. I told him how my husband cries for his father every night and how eagerly he wanted to see him since he knew his dad wasn't doing well.

My husband was vaccinated, so the permission was easily granted and even extended to his daughter and spouse to bid their final goodbye. The following day, he went to the hospital to see his father, following all the precautions. He wore a mask, gloves and got a sanitizer with him. During the visit, my husband face timed us on the phone, so my father-in-law could see his grandkids that he adores. He was trying to talk to us intermittently while catching his breath. I was so heartbroken to see him like that; he had gotten so weak and his skin so pale.

He verbalized that he did not want to die, and I broke down crying. I came to the other room because I did not want my husband to see that; I wanted him to stay strong in that crucial time. Being a nurse, I know what the end of life looks like, but it was so hard for me to deal with. He was out of breath, yet he tried hard to tell us how much he loved us. Then, a nurse came and asked me to leave, saying, "Your period is over, sir."

I replied, "Okay, give me two minutes."

My husband then asked us to say goodbye to him. My kids said, "Love you a lot, grandpa." And my little one gave him a flying kiss which made him smile.

He then waved goodbye to us. My husband waved bye and left the room with a heavy heart and tears in his eyes.

He got home and was super emotional. He got all the old photo albums out, and we recalled all the old memories; he was telling us stories about his father. A little distraction was all he needed, but it only lasted for a while.

Later that night, at approximately 11 p.m., we got a call from the hospital saying that my father-in-law had expired. We shifted him on a ventilator, but his lungs stopped working entirely, and all of a sudden, his heart stopped. I was working that evening when I received that news. I asked my colleagues to cover for me for a few minutes to inform my husband.

I called him, and my lips were shivering; I knew his father was his universe, I knew this news would break him. I said, sorry but your father couldn't make it. He squeaked and asked me to come home. I went to the superior and asked them to give me an early off and explain the whole situation. They were kind and let me go.

I got home, and it was so hard to watch my husband cry like that. He was looking like a tomato, with red eyes and a teary face. I jumped and hugged him, trying to console him. I was there to give him strength, but looking at him sobbing like that made me cry too. That was the first time I had seen my husband cry so much. He was not just crying; his tears were filled with anger, as he was upset about how his father died. He blamed it on the staff, saying it happened because of their negligence and carelessness.

He got tough on himself, and he was like, I didn't do anything for my father, they didn't feed him anything all those days, they killed him. His anger was speaking, not just bitterness; he was disappointed in himself too. I tried to talk him out of it, telling him all the great things he did for him and us. I said your father would be so proud of you, and trust me, he had gone to a better place. A place without suffering and pain; so, don't cry for him; just pray and cherish the moments you shared with him. He smiled while tears were flowing from his eyes.

My father-in-law was undoubtedly the humblest person on the planet. He always had a subtle smile on his face; his personality was very welcoming. I had known him for the past six years, and I had never seen him getting angry or being harsh to someone. He was very much giving, always helping people and caring for others. He brought his children so beautifully as well. My father-in-law loved his family, and he did everything to support them. He never treated me like his son's wife, yet he always made sure that I felt like I was home, always pampering me and treating me like her own daughter. He adored his grandchildren so much that he always brought them gifts and candies whenever he came to our house. Once he got my older one a toy gun, he still had it.

I named my youngest son Seth after he said that he would have given him that name if he had another son. He held an exceptional place in our hearts and our lives. We will surely miss him, especially around the holidays. I will forever envision the spot where he would sit to eat his big pieces of turkey on thanksgiving, the most prominent bone from the rib roast at Christmas dinner, and how he would plunge into his plate as he yelled aloud for his wine to chase it.

My kids would miss him so much because he used to be a kid around them. He played with them, taught them new tricks, and showed them fake magic. My kids deliberately used to wait for him to visit us. My father-in-law happened to be there, and he taught him a lesson, he said: "Not every day would be easy, there would be days when you would feel like not doing anything, but those should be the days when you must prove yourself wrong and face those challenges headstrong." He always came to our house with a big bag full of gifts for his grandsons. He was a man of discipline and value, and that's what he had taught his son and grandsons. My father-in-law always told us never to give up and face the failures, my younger one once fell from his bicycle, and he was crying uncontrollably.

Those words still linger in my head even now. I wish I could have spent more time with you to know how much you mean to us. You had loved life even on your dying bed; you whispered between your breaths that you did not want to die. You were a fighter, and it won't be the same without you, but I hope you will be in a better place now!

Miss you, Pops, sleep in eternal peace; you will forever be in my heart.

CHAPTER 15:

The First Crack in The Glass Home

Where we love is home - home that our feet may leave, but not our hearts. **-Oliver Wendell Holmes, Sr.**

Home is just a beam of four walls or a cemented structure, but these are not the things that make a home; it's the people living in it, it's the family. It's because of the beautiful human beings who turn that structure of cement and plaster into a beautiful house worth residing in. Everyone wants to have a beautiful family, a place which they can call home, and it is heartwarming to lead a life like that with a sweet and caring family, living in a beautiful cozy house like that. But not everyone is blessed with that, and something similar happened to me.

Life is all about wanting and dreaming. You can work towards your goals and have as much you wanted, but it could feel like losing if no one shows interest or pays attention to your consistent hard work, even though I was privileged to be the owner of four houses in America. Two of the houses were rental properties; one was a vacation home, and the other was my permanent marital residence. I rented one of the two families' house to one of my elder cousins because she had nowhere to stay, and I couldn't see her in such a devastated and helpless state; so, I rented the house to her.

She had no one to look after her and no place to go on top of that. I just wanted to help her, so I gave her permission to live in the house until she had a job and could afford the rent. We came up with this plan to start paying the current rent and gradually catch up with her past rent. She agreed to it but later contradicted herself and declined to fulfill her obligation. Even she refused to pay the gas or light bills. She lived for free for 1 ½ year and didn't pay a penny.

Later, when I was considering selling the house, I told her that she must move and search for some other place to live. She got upset with me and made me her biggest enemy. Although she was working, she did not pay me a single cent, and the irony was; after leaving my house and finding another apartment, she was paying there. She couldn't pay me because, according to her, she wasn't earning a lot; but now, all of a sudden, she started making good and can pay the rent.

I also endured more traumatic experiences from my other tenants. One of them owed me eight months of rent, and to crown it all, she came up which clever excuses but always made promises to pay. She continued living there with section 8 paying 20 percent, and she also had to pay the remainder. The tenant got infuriated when I asked her for my money. I mean, I couldn't understand why people gave such vile reactions. You live in my house, and when I ask for the rent, you call me your enemy and I turn out to be the wrong person?

One day, I received a call from the same tenant stating that she was just out from the hospital after being admitted for a hypoglycemia coma. She continuously sobbed and begged to cook dinner for her, as she had to eat medicines. I felt so sorry for her, made some soup and curry for her and immediately left my house to give her food. I kept doing so for the next two weeks. I felt if I did not help her, I would have been guilty about myself, that even after looking at someone in such an awful condition, I didn't give a helping hand.

She used all of my good qualities, niceness, and caring nature, and when it came to showing it from her end, there was nothing. Even I wasn't expecting some great grand gestures of kindness from her, just my rent. But she was always reluctant and continued making all the excuses in the world and refused to pay her rent, and I ended up emptying my bank account to fund the mortgage. I took her to court, but I did not receive anything up to date. I eventually got her evicted. Due to her shortcoming and the long process involved with eviction, I lost both properties. Today, together with my current husband, I owned two properties.

Marriage

Marriage happens as with cages; the birds without despair to get in, and those within despair of getting out. *-Montaigne*

Marriage is a sacred process; it is about two different individuals accepting each other with flaws and mistakes while promising to stand by each other till their last breath. Mostly, promises are made to be broken, and in the same way, some marriage also meets their tragic end.

For the longest, I thought I had the best marriage, having the best person like my husband, my first love. I think this would have been the best time to recall the time when we tied that knot, and we repeated the marital vows, "till death do us part." Once upon a time in our relationship, I think he fitted under the title of the world's best husband, and I felt that I had the best relationship; most importantly, best married life, and to top that, the best family. We were so happy with each other; he was the Pooh to my Batty Most individuals used to give me great compliments about my relationship with my former husband, as they used to see us living and loving each other so much. Some also seek my advice on strengthening a relationship and keeping the spark alive.

Even though my formal husband had extra-marital affairs at the initial phase of our marriage, I moved past that and looked for a brighter future. Not until one night when I got a dream that he was being unfaithful again, and I talked to him about this dream, as I was growing anxious. Nevertheless, he laughed first and denied it all, saying it was just a dream. I believed him and asked God for a revelation.

His mother also told me that she saw a brown-skinned girl performing witchcraft in my marriage during the said time. She said that girl wanted to break you both up, so be cautious. My mother-in-law also asked me if I had a friend with that skin tone? I replied yes. Then she advised me to stay away from her for my good and save my marriage. I immediately ended the friendship with her to save my marriage. I also became more religious, started praying, and grew more connected to God. The woman of God also told me that I should be careful with my older siblings as they are jealous of their close relationship with their family. I would socialize with my family, but always in fear and doubt. One of my former husband's uncles died suddenly around the Christmas season. Traveling to Guyana during the Christmas holidays was difficult, as last-minute flights were expensive and harder to find. But, being in a close-knitted family, expensive flights were not an issue. The most important thing is the whole family being present for the burial and providing their support. My former husband's job had much flexibility, so work was not an issue either. Hence, he decided to travel before us to start making the burial arrangements.

He traveled on a first-class flight and was able to take additional luggage. During his travel, he met the person he is currently married to. Sometime around the journey, he must have written that woman's name, address, and telephone number on a piece of paper. He accidentally dropped this piece of paper in the room where we were staying in Linden. While cleaning that room, I found that piece of paper and got blank for a minute.

I was weirded out, and all negative thoughts were rushing into my mind. I hid that note in the suitcase, later I confronted him about it, and I told his family about the malicious act of infidelity. He didn't even seem guilty, and on the same night, I searched for that paper and removed it from the spot I was keeping it in. I was out of words for his hideous act, but I was glad I memorized the name and address from that note, except the phone number. After the burial, all his family members gathered together in Linden as we celebrated the holiday while in grief. My former husband lifted himself and left, stating that he would meet some of his friends.

Even his brother and parents said they wanted to have a conversation with him, but he said that this was important and left. I was tearful, and I sat there uneasy, in disbelief, while his mother tried to console me. I knew that the trust was shaken up, and that was the first crack in the glass of my marriage.

I asked my cousin who lived in Linden about the girl even provided her the address. But she did not know anything about her. Likewise, one of his sisters stated, "When you find a number like these, you make duplicate copies." I told her that this caught me by surprise, and I was traumatized.

I lost my thinking capabilities, and my heart was not beating normally; I was blank. I did not have another conversation with him while in Guyana. As I got back home to New Jersey, I moved downstairs and began sleeping in the guest room and kept in silence. We did not communicate that whole time; a silence had wrapped upon us. The only thing that we talked about was the kids, and that too, only rarely.

My formal husband did not want to end our marriage, and he begged for forgiveness. He cried in front of me, said sorry like a million times, and promised that it wouldn't happen again. I did forgive him, and things slowly started getting back to normal. But during the rest of the time in the marriage, I was always in fear, mistrust, and pain. Every time I looked at this man, I was filled with disappointment; at times, I tore since I was working two jobs, raising a family while advancing my education to keep our family afloat. Later, something gave me the courage and I took a stand for myself. I decided not to take no for an answer and fully opened my heart while placing infidelity behind my back. I thought our marriage was back on track and built on a more solid platform. Not until we left for my brother's marriage. Even though I did not have extra cash then, I assisted my brother with his wedding and secretly extended and remodeled the house of my former husband's parents' home that was going to be handed down to us. I was indecisive about going due to not having enough money for the travel, but then I finally decided to go because my brother was getting married, and I did not want to miss it.

The date was decided, but I did not buy my ticket since I had to pay all the mortgages and wait for the other paycheck. My former husband did not ask about our tickets or travel arrangements but went ahead and booked his ticket two days ahead of the set dates and left us behind.

We did partake in the health fair and my brother's wedding, after which my former husband was anxious to go back to Linden to complete his vacation. He left and went out a few times during his stay without asking me to join. He also booked his returned flight a few days after the original dates without sharing it with me. I was disturbed and immediately knew he was up to something.

As I returned home, his mother stayed with me. I recapped his behaviors, and she said she would talk to him. I just knew that some things couldn't change and old habits don't have a stop button; I was crying out to God and questioning why. When he returned, his entire persona changed; he began screaming during most conversations. I asked him to complete the painting at one of our rentals since I already had payment from section 8 and the tenant wanted to move in. He grew mad and started shouting; I had a tongue lashing from his loud foul words. After that, he told me not to talk or tell him anything about the rentals and said that I was raising his blood pressure; I realized that I could not hold another conversation with him.

I realized that this man hated me from that moment, and I kept it to myself while spending long days and nights crying. I decided to apply and start my doctoral program to clear my thoughts. Since we were not speaking unless it was about the kids, I availed my spare time to advance my knowledge. I used to stay up most of the nights studying and writing my papers in the room while he was on the porch or his computer, bombarding the place with loud music. We stayed in bed, but I used pillows to separate us.

One night he came into the room, sucked his teeth, and yelled at me for being in bed with my books and papers. I immediately moved out and went into the guest room and never returned. For two years, this is how we were living. As usual, I continued to cook, clean, and do laundry, hoping that he would appreciate all of the things that I was doing and seek another pardon. We attended church but never sat together and even drove in separate cars. A colossal drift was created between us.

At the end of the year, his family planned to go to Atlanta to spend the Christmas holiday. I did not go since it was my turn to work and be on call during the weekend. Likewise, he was not talking to me, and I would not drive in the same car with him. So, he went alone.

On his return from Atlanta, it was the first day of the year; although being sick, I cooked the food he liked. There was still a minor chord of hope within me. As a few days went by, I asked him about us. Per his words, "you are a wicked witch; I would not even crawl on the floor and beg for you." His tone grew darker, "I prefer to dig a hole in the ground and bury you." That was enough for me, and I couldn't handle it anymore. I used it as my turning point, and I knew that I would not stay in a relationship feeling insulted and unwanted.

I immediately called his older brother and told him everything he said to me. I was hoping that he would understand. Instead, that hope turned into astonishment when he took his side. He said, "He is my only brother; even though he is wrong, I will stick by his side one hundred percent." I was in a state of shock as I was always kind to him; I would ensure that he ate a good meal during his stay at my house. I ensured that his visit was spent in comfort, and he had to say this? I felt like a bird with a broken wing, in extreme pain, but no one would listen and help.

I was endlessly crying, with my former husband's words playing on a loop in my mind. I was helpless, with no one to talk to from the center of his life to a vague memory. The love of my life was snatched from me, leaving me scattered in a million little pieces.

CHAPTER 16:

Family

Family is the complete source of support – a place where you are accepted and never judged—people who will have your back no matter what. You can always crawl in your mother's lap when things go south. You can always rely on your father to help you make sense of the world around you and sort out anything that may be troubling you mentally. Your siblings can be your support system when the whole world is against you because they are your safe space.

People owe a lot of their success and triumphs to their families because they can be at your side selflessly and relentlessly. When the going gets tough, and you have no one to fall back on, it is your family that helps you sustain the blows that life struggles might strike you with. That's the power of the family, being there for each other no matter what. But it isn't always glittery and fun for a family; they all go through their fair share of ups and downs.

The whole thing that had happened with my husband left me shattered. It broke my heart into a million pieces and destroyed my family. It was very traumatic for Mary and Melanie, and they were pretty hurt, witnessing all of the tension going on in our home. While we had a heated argument, Mary left the house and walked while crying around the neighborhood. In their innocent minds, they did not know what was exactly going on, and that's why I did not discuss it with them, as it was too much for those little souls.

I hid my feelings for years so that the girls would continue to be nurtured by both of their parents. I knew they sensed every change in emotions between their father and me. They would hate to see me locked up inside the room; I made it look like I was doing my school work. As they greeted me, I put on a plastic smile and quickly dried my tear, and smoothed the frogging wrinkles from my face.

My little one wasn't so old when the family was going on this devastating loop, and once out of her innocence, she asked if their dad was going crazy and why he was behaving like that. A rift was created between them too, which wasn't suitable for those kids. Later, when we parted ways, his girlfriend started living with him, and my daughters went to stay with him for the weekend; they would greet her, and she would call him and report all wrong things about them. She never really liked them and lied blatantly, trying to make him against them.

On one occasion, while Melanie was spending a weekend with her dad, she accidentally dropped the phone in the water while washing her hair; she placed it in a bowl of rice, left it in her room there by mistake, and returned home. Her stepmother found it and called her father, telling him that I send obeah to the house. He called both of our girls screaming at them; even though they told him what happened, he didn't believe his daughter.

He moved this woman into our marital home without my permission, and his family allowed this to happen while it all was profoundly affecting the kids. My daughters were so fearful of this woman at first; at times, they did not want to visit their dad just because they didn't like to see her and tried to avoid her. I continuously instilled in my girls to be respectful to her and ensure they leave the house tidy before coming home.

It was deplorable for my girls as they say that they do not feel the love from the paternal side of the family anymore. I still encourage them to call their grandparents, aunts, uncles, and cousins. Due to this break-up, I struggled on my own, ensured that their needs were being fulfilled, and tried my best to provide them with everything.

Their father stopped supporting them after I left, but he gave them a couple of dollars when he saw them. He paid half of their school fees but never asked how we lived and if we had a bed to sleep on. I am incredibly grateful that I earned enough to provide for them.

It was unbelievable to see a family that was closely knitted and grew up in a God-fearing home would let my girls suffer and lead to not having their father support them. It is more so disgraceful to tell others that their father doesn't even take care of them. Whenever there would be an event, he always made promises, but he was the master of breaking them too.

The only thing he used to do was to pay their fees, and lately, he wasn't even doing that on time; the school used to give us notices, and then he would send the money. Additionally, when Melanie turned 16, we threw her a sweet 16 party in which we were supposed to split the bill; but he didn't even bother to pay a penny; he started to act as if he barely knew me. I did not fight but took care of it, yet he blamed me for his family members not attending the party. I thank God that my girls are older now, see, and understand each and everything. I often tried to shield their father by focusing on all the positive things and their life during the marriage. If there would be an event, he reluctantly shies away from taking pictures together, not putting into the perspective that this is a symbol of the kids showcasing their parents. I did not know that this was the same man I married and loved; he changed drastically. He made our lives hell and created this nightmare for us.

Despite knowing what led to the divorce, my husband had all of these extramarital affairs and emotionally abused me; I was pinned of being the cheater. My mother-in-law attempted to destroy my integrity although, her family members reminded her about her son's relationship. Additionally, she tried to lie to my siblings, defending her son. At first, they believed, not until I showed them the evidence, and that's when they realized what was exactly going on.

We all know that there will be a day for judgment coming if you are religious. I was crucified for leaving; and told that love comes from God. My faith was tested, and before I stayed in that relationship and went completely crazy, I prioritized myself and ran from that relationship. I did not have a plan, nor did I know this strength existed. What I knew was that it wouldn't be the will of God to see me suffering, so that grew some amount of hope that God was there to take care of me.

Even though, after the divorce, I did not hate his family, I continued to value the good times we shared. I would always remind my kids that we have had experienced a good time together. But as much respect I still had for them, it wasn't like that from their side; they would be keeping an eye on me and would be eagerly waiting to see me fall. Thanks to God, I continued to strive, and he watched over me.

While ending my relationship with him, he cursed me for being a white man's slave. But I didn't want him to bad-mouth me again; I confronted him with facts about his wife and told him that you had this hole inside you that you could never fill.

He had also manipulated the girls against me; I had to tell them the truth about his current relationship since he attempted to crucify me by telling the girls lies. I did not save the evidence to show them, but I let my family tell them the truth.

Moving On - My Dating Life

After leaving him, I thought it would be easy to move on in my life and get it back in the flow. I thought dating was going to be easy. I had no other choice but to search for someone online since I could hardly find time to go out or know any friends who would set me up with someone. I didn't plan to go on those dating sites, but once I was with my cousin and had this deep conversation, she suggested I move on with my life and start searching for someone online. I was very skeptical at first; later, I found an online dating advertisement while looking for a house. I finally decided to explore it, although I still had second thoughts.

I was happy when I got into the site named "Christian mingles." I met a respectable inventor who claimed to fear God. I was so enthralled since finding a Christian guy who was not married at such age was challenging. I questioned the credibility, and with some skepticism, I gave it a try and started chatting with this guy. After a few days, we shared telephone numbers and spent countless hours talking on the phone a couple of times each day.

This guy blew my mind when he said, "God sent you to be the right time. " I thought it was so real as it was coming from a Christian. We decided to meet at Barnes and Noble. I was not a coffee drinker then, so I sipped on tea as we chatted. I did not feel the connections. This guy lied about his age, and he looked older than what he said. I was uncomfortable to be around him, but I still gave it a chance saying that age does not define a person.

After knowing he lied, I had to be confident and have a full investigation to see what I could find out before falling in love and hurting myself. After knowing his full name which I asked to add his number under his profile, I decided to delve deeper into the details. The information retrieved was that other women created a chat room under this guy's business portfolio and rated him as an entrepreneur. Some were scornful; they went as far as inviting other women to connect telephonically on a platform to share personal information. I was embarrassed to know that the devil was also mingling on the site, and I was extremely put off by him.

During this time, I also happened to go back on the site to confirm if it was the same guy as I could not believe it all. While it was all happening, I did not hear from him for four days. I did not question it as he told me that he was travelling abroad on a business trip with limited correspondence, but he will find a way to communicate with me. He also said he wanted to invite me but thought it would be too soon, as we had just met.

I couldn't make my mind about him, whether to trust him or not. As I did not hear from this man for several days, I decided to visit the site to see if he had shown up there. I couldn't believe what I saw; he was active on the site. I immediately messaged him. He immediately called and apologized for being back on the site. At the same time, he told me I got back on the site to respond to the messages of other women out of courtesy. That was when I fitted all the pieces together and mixed it with the other women's additional information and told him to keep doing it, and I blocked him.

He kept mingling with other women; although he occasionally sent me messages, he realized that I lost interest as I never responded to any of his messages. A few months had gone by, and I didn't receive any messages from him, but this time he texted me from a different number to invite me to his house as he was having a barbeque and pool party at his residence. I did not respond, making it crystal clear that I did not want any connection with him. He left me alone after that silent treatment that I gave him. It did not stop me from online dating; I was even more motivated but had different strategies. Firstly, I quit Christian mingle because I thought those men were not God-fearing and total liars. I hoped that the men on this site would fear the Lord, and we could have something in common (being religious by following and living as per the biblical principles). Although I did match and talked to some good-looking men (from their outer appearance), I later realized that they are the epitome of liars.

Their conversations may start with God's goodness and end with God's blessing, but their action would be completely opposite. Some of the lies include seeking a soul mate, and that they want to start a family, but later it would be all about them seeking pleasures. And not just lies; some used to create fake profiles and catfish people.

The whole journey of online dating had its pros and cons. There are some good men out there, but everyone needs to be careful and know the guys entirely before you can think of exchanging numbers. I went as far as doing a background check before sharing my number or personal information. Nonetheless, this did not detour me; I still did not give up until I assigned myself to another site called Zoosk, where I met my current husband.

CHAPTER 17:
Almost Losing My Life

Life is quite unpredictable and uncertain; it is kind of similar to the weather; you don't know what's going to happen the next minute. One moment it could be super-hot, with the sun glaring its hotness; the next, it could be raining. Hence, you can't foresee what life has gotten for you; you just have to wait and witness it. Life doesn't always feel good, and at times we don't value it until something dreadful happens, and it changes our perspective.

It was a beautiful morning on April 29th, but not very pleasing for me as I woke up with an unbearable headache; the pain was so severe that I couldn't get standstill. I took out the B.P operator, checked my blood pressure, and I didn't notice any unusual measurement; it was all normal. As it was fine, I did not take any pain medication, but I knew something was wrong. As a medical provider, I knew that this could be pre-eclampsia as I was pregnant. I did not have any other symptoms that accompanied it, but I called my doctor just for caution. My doctor was busy with a delivery, so I got a call back from another doctor, and he told me to rush to the hospital immediately and get myself checked in the maternity ward.

I hopped into the shower, dressed up, and went to Nyack hospital. The secretary at the hospital offered me a seat, asked for my identification and insurance card. I took it out of my wallet, handed it to her, and asked for a seat. The nurse had a quick check-up, asked me about my condition, reviewed my symptoms, immediately placed me on the bed, and hooked me up to a monitor. The nurse monitored my heart rate and ran some tests; later, the doctor came; it was the same one I had called. He told me they would have to take me to the operating room to deliver the baby. I asked them about my doctor? And he was not on duty that day, so I didn't wait for him and got on terms with the new doctor as the baby's heart rate dropped.

I was scared, I didn't know what would happen next, but all I knew was that I could pray. Hence, during this whole time of terror and agony, I began to pray aloud and asked God for my life to be a testimony, which will draw men unto God after telling them about God's faithfulness. I prayed to the nurses, doctors, scrub technicians, anesthesiologists, and all those who will be partaking in my surgery. Additionally, I prayed for the baby in utero that God would strengthen his heartbeat and protect him from all the dangers, and introduce this kid to the world with great health. I did not foresee what would happen to me, but as usual, I committed my life into God's everlasting hands.

I was shifted into the operating room; I got an epidural, and out came my handsome baby boy. After the baby was taken out from my uterus, I overheard the doctor asking for a specific drug to cauterize one of my blood vessels, but it was unavailable. Nevertheless, a substitute drug was used, and I was sent to the recovery room for constant monitoring. While in the recovery room, I was allowed to take a few ice chips. I was given a few, but those ice chips were the best, so I begged my husband to fill the glass and bring it. I have had about two drinks of those ice chips and yet wanted more.

I asked for another glass of it and stuffed it in my mouth. Not long after, my husband noticed that my eyes turned upwards, and I had gotten extremely pale. He glanced at the monitor and noticed that my blood pressure was dropping. He immediately rang for the nurse, who later came and gave me a bolus of intravenous fluid.

He also tried to wake me up by this time, but I couldn't regain consciousness, and my blood pressure continued to drop. He kept ringing the bell for the nurse, but she was unresponsive, he ran out to the nurses' station to get her, but no one was there. He yelled along the hallway and banged on multiple doors until he saw the nurse who was supposed to be monitoring me come out of the break room. After my husband told her the entire situation, she ran to my room, and I was unconsciously lying there. She dialed a number through the phone in the ward, and the rapid response team arrived within minutes.

I was in and out of consciousness. I remembered feeling severe pain while my uterus was being massaged. While specific tests were taken and I had multiple blood transfusions hanging, my stat hemoglobin returned, and they were deficient, like my platelets. I went into disseminated intravascular coagulation (DIC), which means that my blood was not clotting, so I continued to bleed.

After a while, I heard the doctors screaming at my husband to sign the consent form so that they could take me to the operating room again. I was in extreme pain, and as I gained consciousness again, they were talking about consent, so I told them that I had already signed the papers; the first consent covers this one as well, as it's an entailed a complication from the previous surgery. I had tubes and wires hanging all over my arms while an oxygen mask was fabricated on my face. I was crushing with pain and begged to get my uterus removed immediately. I had a feeling something terrible was about to happen, so I was just praying and asking God for a miracle.

During this crucial time, my husband was pacing the hospital units and calling all of my friends and his friends to be with him at the hospital. They all came out and were there with us in such a hard time. The second surgery was successful. However, I was intubated and placed in a medically induced coma; since I was edematous from multiple fluids and blood products sources. I was sent to the intensive care unit with a grave disposition.

My husband did not leave my side, even though he was not allowed to stay in the intensive care unit, but he was determined and told them he would not leave since they almost killed me and he wouldn't take the risk again. The hospital had no other choice but to bend their rules and allow him to be by my side. He slept on the floor for two nights until a recliner was given to him for the rest of the stay. He did not bathe or brush his teeth and ate whatever food the cafeteria had.

A few days later, I was awakened from the medically induced coma; and was preparing to be extubated; as the team rounded, they cheered for me. I couldn't understand any of that, so I asked why are they cheering like that for me, and they told me that they did not believe I was going to survive since all who suffered from what I went through ended up dying. I immediately began to boast about the goodness of my God and encourage them to serve and trust in him. It must be another testing of my faith. Through it all, God has been great.

My abdomen had gotten so big after giving birth in 2019. It was super bull Sunday 2020, a few days before my birthday; I looked at my stomach and said, I have to start working out at home and should do some sit-ups. I began exercising, doing squats and sit-ups. Soon after, I began to feel minor abdominal pain. I decided to take a shower and nap before my shift. After showering, the pain intensified, I ignored it and tried to nap, but the pain kept growing more and more. I turned and twisted myself but could not get comfortable; the pain did not stop.

I called my boss and told her I could not work my shift and told her my condition. As I got to the emergency room at Good Samaritan hospital, I was immediately placed into a cubicle. It was so uncomfortable; I leaned across the back of a chair to splint the area. The Nurse Practitioner arrived and prescribed the pain medication. As the nurse pushed the medication, I felt as if my body was being cut open and as though I would fall out of the bed. I grabbed the rails and told the nurse; I did not want another dose of this drug. The pain eased; I went for a C.T scan. After a while, the pain intensified again; I begged for half of the dose since I was scared after the first dose.

A few days before my birthday, I had the surgical correction; it developed some complications that caused me to stay nine days in the hospital. The surgeon later came to see me and showed the C.T scan results, and I was admitted with an intestinal obstruction and a ventral hernia. A nasogastric tube and intravenous were placed, and I could not consume anything through my mouth. On my first post-operative day, the surgeon visited and went over the surgical procedure. It took him a total of seven hours to complete my surgery, which usually takes two hours.

He asked me how I was even able to live? My intestines were outside of my abdominal cavity. I told him I live by the faith and that faith came from believing in God. I said this is another testing of my trust; I did not give up on God, and I never will. These obstacles drew me even more closely to him. In each step of the way, I held on to the ever-loving arms of God, as I know he held my future in his palms. My pastor came right over after he found out that I was admitted, and we began praying and reaching out to God, not only for me but for my roommate too, who was a Christian. As they say, asking from God never goes down in vain, another miracle happened, and my surgery was successful.

Regaining my strength

When I was given another chance at life, I got more connected to God. I used to spend immeasurable hours praying to God, fasting, and asking for His guidance. Always seeking love from God, I envisioned a circle with no beginning and no ending and was highly inspired by that. I often started reading the Bible, seeking scriptures to soothe my aches. Some include Psalm 139:10 "If I take the wings of the morning, and dwell in the uttermost part of the sea; Even there shall thy hand lead me, and thy right hand shall hold me."

Colossians 1:17 "And he is before all things, and by him, all things consists."

Each day was like a new beginning. I would take a deep breath, smile, and dive into it, headstrong. I was comforted as I remember that God woke me up for a reason; I should trust in him as he always has a plan for us. But I was going through a slippery slope around that time; I couldn't understand my emotions; one moment I used to be happy, the other I was crying. I did feel at peace; there was always a thought bugging me. Around everyone, I used to put up a plastic smile, but I was in dismay of anyone finding out the pain or how I was suffering internally.

As I entered work, school, gym, or the grocery store, I put on the happy feeling. Meanwhile, I was pouring barrels of tears from the inside. I couldn't convey what I was feeling; I was ashamed how that professional woman who is so much in love with her family, cooks well, cleans well, and the person who loves humanity would be going through this.

I did not know how to break my bruised and bleeding heart; so, I kept silent. I was engulfed in my inner feeling and did not even open up to my family or friends. I always looked on the good side, always hoping that things would work themselves out. Just to help myself, I have decided to join a gym, and I got a personal trainer.

During this time, I was really at my lowest. It was so hard to find that escape; I felt very trapped as I was always dependent on my former husband for almost everything. Even for the smallest things, be it taking my car for service, washing my car, flying to the airport as I always, etc.

I started investigating the things that made me sad and then the things that excited me and created an equilibrium, especially when my kids were around. It was hard to think when you had lost your self-esteem, but I could not allow that to overcrowd my feelings or continue to be engulfed in that state. I decided to focus on my sanity, to dive into hope by eradicating all the negative emotions. I painted all the pictures of negativity with cheerful, bright colors in my head.

I adorned myself in my lily-white lab coat and stepped in my high heels while looking after my patients and doing a clinical rotation with my students in the evening at the hospital. Everyone in the hospital loved me. I enjoyed the crowd cheering—what a beautiful soul. The staff and families at the facilities applauded me for the quality care I delivered to receiving cards with pleasing commentaries and words of gratitude from my students. I used the echo of those powerful words to replace the negative ones since that was controlling me.

Those responses played a crucial role in dispensing my day at work in any given situation. They became my theme through the process for the day. I allowed the positivity to take over, letting it control my reaction and decision-making capabilities. Next, I was more eager to succeed. I was pressed on to complete my Doctoral degree as I was looking for a prestigious title. Being addressed as a doctor was one of the most fulfilling moments as I escaped the harness of being called a wicked witch. At first, when I was called Dr. Boggi, I quickly answered with that condescending gesture and was hard to accommodate swiftly and responded.

For some time, as I acknowledged and reached this level of my education, my decision-making capabilities improved in both my personal and professional life. I felt a sense of empowerment and the drive to share my story and reach the world. It gives me the courage and energy to build on lasting relationships. I am strengthened to create a forum for my students who are walking this path and looking for an escape. Some of whom entrusted me and asked me to be their mentor.

As I navigated along the path of recovery in my daily routine, I was encouraging some of my students on the importance of higher education and how to become successful in their careers. I just don't know how this conversation initiated at times, but somehow it came out with a super smooth transition from talking to them about their career path to escaping your trapped emotions. These daily interactions fashioned my growth and strengthened my well-being as I overcame my trapped emotion. I felt more like an advocate who is now offering peer support.

I am a strong advocate and believe in assisting others experiencing these emotions on how to lead onto this road to escape. I realized that I had more to give when some of my students called me Mommy-teacher and asked me to share my stories and how they told me how people could benefit from them. How individuals can learn and feel empowered from my experiences and that never giving up attitude.

CHAPTER 18:

Taking Care of Myself and My Spirituality

Spirituality is how you can find meaning in your life – a purpose. There are many ways to find spirituality, but for me, religion works perfectly. The values and principles provided in our scriptures aid me in living my life with God standing beside me throughout every step I take. I know it is difficult to prove this, but spirituality is definitely related to one's mental health. Our body, mind, and spirit are intertwined, and positive beliefs through faith can provide us with spiritual healing and comfort.

Likewise, to step up my faith: I continued to read the Bible and intercede with my maker, easing the gathering with my brothers and sisters in our Lord and savior.

COVID had unexpectedly struck our lives, impacting our daily routines, and the effects of this pandemic on religion were manifold. Our government had imposed plenty of restrictions due to social distancing, after which all the gatherings in the places of faith took a sharp halt. During the lockdown, churches and Sunday school remained closed, but luckily for me, these practices moved online.

Due to the troubles brought by this pandemic, I often joined several religious services virtually and connected with my pastor whenever I needed prayers and spiritual guidance. Similarly, I always turned to the

Bible scriptures that healed and offered strength to me. Many instances led to some scriptures becoming my personal favorite: Once, I held on to God's promise, the vision He showed me when I was a young girl, that He holds my future in the palm of His hand and that He will never fail me.

I, then, reminded God of His promises, knowing that He said through His word: *the Lord is a mighty tower, where his people can run into for safety* (proverbs 18:10). I also remained reassured because the steadfast love of the LORD never ceases; His mercies never come to an end, and they are new every morning: *great is your faithfulness* (lamentation 3:22-23).

Then, I was reminded of another scripture that I should "lift my eye unto the hill, from whence cometh my help. My help cometh from the Lord, which made heaven and earth" *(Psalms 121:1-2). And in 1 Peter 5:7 is the most reassuring scripture for me,* "Casting all your anxieties on Him because he cares for you."

I knew that God would raise me again, as I repeated the scripture: "Now to him who can do immeasurably more than all we ask or imagine, according to his power that is at work within us." *(Ephesians 3:20)*

Re-reading these scriptures whenever I feel down is essential in my life because it provides me with the direction that I need. They give me hope and tell me what I should be doing and what I should not be doing. Not only do they provide me with spiritual protection, but the scriptures are like guidelines for every problem in my life.

Another scripture that I have read before has recently become more relatable to me as I add it to my go-to bible verses, Isaiah 40:31, "But they who wait for the LORD shall renew their strength; they shall mount up with wings like eagles; they shall run and not be weary; they shall walk and not faint?"

At times when I felt low, I would read Deuteronomy 31:6, "Be strong and courageous. Do not be afraid or terrified because of them, or the LORD your God goes with you; he will never leave you nor forsake you". *Along with Psalm 27:12,* "The LORD is my light and my salvation; whom shall, I fear? The LORD is the stronghold of my life; of whom shall I be afraid". *Then, in John 4:18,* "There is no fear in love. But perfect love drives out fear because fear has to do with punishment. The one who fears is not made perfect in love".

As I began fasting and praying repeatedly, I remembered this scripture that I used to say as a memory verse when I went for the evening Sunday school class from Romans 8:31, "*If God is for us, who can be against us?*"

It dispelled all my fears knowing that my spiritual food is fulfilling, and I could continue to be strengthened when Romans 15:13 reminded me that "The God of hope fill you with all joy and peace as you trust in him, so that you may overflow with hope by the power of the Holy Spirit." *And Psalm 31:24 instructs me to* "Be strong, and let your heart take courage, all you who wait for the LORD."

As the flashbacks of my emotions emerged, I often referred to 1 Peter 5:7, "*Casting all your anxieties on him because he cares for you.*" I also remembered one of my pastor's teachings, in which he described how Christians could overcome their worldly desires. He reminded me that I only need to put my trust in God when he quoted the Philippians 4:19, "*And my God will supply every need of yours according to his riches in glory in Christ Jesus.*"

Nothing I desired could compare to what God can do for me. I referred to my spirituality and allowed it to take precedence, knowing that the deity of a higher power is in control. My fundamental nourishments provided me with some of the most valuable and powerful tools that always came handy. And whenever I was feeling weak and discouraged, I read Philippians 4:13, "*I can do all things through him who strengthens me.*"

Along with my spiritual help, I realized that I needed to do more to bring myself up. The feelings of low self-esteem were trying to overcrowd me. I did not feel comfortable seeking psychosocial treatment because I did not want to be labeled. Yet again, I took another leap of faith and used this recipe that I created to help myself.

First and foremost, I had to recognize that I was suffering. I did not want to continue in the same state of mind day after day. It was vital for me to acknowledge that this would send me to a mental institution and leave me with major depression if I did not work on it. Mainly because low self-esteem was engulfing my life after a while and becoming a part of my daily life rituals. I went wrong when I started feeding onto this feeling by acting on it every day, to the extent where my children began to recognize my state of mind and how overwhelmed I was. Seeing their mother that way affected their own emotions, which I could not stand. I needed a new plan, and I needed to change.

The next thing I did was acknowledge the potential complications that this might cause. I did not want to start on psychotropic medication. I was already experiencing sleepless nights and had pent-up tension, leading me to feel anxious over every little thing, which was very different from my usual disposition. Not only this, I was locking myself in separate rooms and distancing myself from my family. I dogged phone calls from my close friend because I felt that the hint of sadness in my voice would tell my story. Often, I would distance myself from even going to dinner just because I wanted to hide my weight loss and because I was afraid that my feelings might show whenever I felt lost in the clouds.

The feeling of withdrawal was always trying to step in; I would always make sure that the door to the guest bedroom was locked by slamming it hard enough to ensure that it was tightly fitted into the notch so that it was completely secured. The lights were always off, the curtains always drawn, to cover the windows so that no bright light from our beautiful atmosphere seeps into the room. I also started snapping at my kids over minor things. Apart from that, I was drastically losing weight – more like dropping pounds by the weeks.

After some time, I decided to go to the gym to strengthen my body even though the trainer was pushing me beyond my limits. My appetite started to subside, but I would force myself to drink smoothies, thinking they were easier to digest. On some days, I would look at food as though it was poison – I had no desire for the foods I used to enjoy. After all, there was no energy left in me to even lift the spoon to feed myself.

After assessing the potential impact of my emotions, I decided to take a step back to help myself get better. I began identifying the triggers that affected my feelings; this allowed me to understand myself and make a list, starting from the trigger that occurred most frequently: to break that down, I made a list of what made me cry the most to the least. After that, I wondered which ones caused me anxiety and which filled me with hatred. These two priorities reflect how my former husband cheated and lied, apart from calling me names that degraded my character.

There is one question that I repeatedly asked myself: do I want to take authority? Although it may sound silly to some, I had to ask myself this question and then find an answer to it immediately. I felt that if my answer to this question were a no, I would remain in the same place and would not have to take another step. If my answer were a yes, I knew I had to put my best foot forward and have a lot of work to do. I tried to make excuses to avoid answering the question and would always run away from it.

However, I knew I had to start finding the answers. After answering yes, I would develop the guidelines for taking authority in certain situations. These guidelines were inspired by my experience of taking care of my residents – care, from a psychological standpoint. I reverted from all the pharmacophoric agents due to the additional side effects they may be causing. Sometimes, I would intrude into some of the conversations the psychologist would ask my residents as though she was asking me, and I answered silently. I looked forward to the goals that she set forth for my residents and assessed them to see if any were applicable. When I was not available during the signing of these care plans, I unconsciously mirrored the goals, worried that my goals may not be materialized within a specific time frame.

To ensure that my targeted goals were met, I would follow up with another question: what am I feeling now? This was done to determine if the set goals were being worked upon or not. It is not uncommon for some plans to not work out. Some goals may be short-termed and others long-termed. At times, I lied to myself and told myself that I was happy since I did not want to be disappointed despite making efforts, neither did I want to seem like a failure. But I reminded myself that I can expect failure and that it is alright to fail, as long as I work even harder the next time.

To begin working harder, I had to determine if the real causes of my emotions were identified. As the ones I kept selecting may not have been the correct ones, it could be possible that I was holding back from identifying the real reasons why I was feeling that way to avoid the entire situation altogether. When they were identified correctly, I developed a concise plan to interrupt those feelings. I told myself that it is not uncommon to hold back all these feelings, but if I do not correctly identify these emotions, they would only prolong my illness – and that is something I did not want to go through.

Some of the goals that I made naturally had to be revised. So, I developed two goals with interventions: long-termed and short-termed. I ensured that my goals were realistic to target them quickly with some simple interventions. Affixed to my interventions were contingency plans and occasional revisions to original plans to hit my target dates. I wanted to ensure that a backup was always there, although I did not anticipate failures.

My journey included documenting all my triggers in a special diary with dates assigned and the next step that I had to take. It was not an easy talk to know, and at times, I was teary while writing. Sometimes, I wrote everything down in my diary and then crossed them out. It was challenging to put them on paper while reflecting on them so profoundly; I was in disbelief. As I discovered the ones I wanted to focus on, memories and flashbacks of these moments crept in. As I reminisced and traced back to when things started going downhill, my mind began to wander. I still could not wrap my head around everything that happened.

Once I went through this step and was satisfied with the results, I proceeded to the next step: focusing on all of the possibilities that exacerbated these triggers. I put my total concentration on them and decided that those were the ones I would focus on. Not just that, but I also questioned myself to determine what the specific circumstances in each event were. Typically, I doubted myself to shy away from the harsh ones. Despite my resistance, I concentrated on the selected triggers and began pondering over them in-depth as I jotted down all the possible ways through which I think they can be controlled. Some seemed hard, while others were difficult to manage. Altogether, I came up with current and future that I can use to manage them. In my journal, I prioritized the most important trigger. Sometimes, it wasn't easy to come up with the first one, but after I discovered it, the others were easily identified. Sometimes, it required me to step away, take a break, and return to work. I often hesitated as I could not afford to lose sight of the most important trigger, so I started taking deep breaths and thinking hard about it. I remember asking myself: Is this the right one? I knew that I was shying away from the harsh reality.

Then, I started numbering the triggers numerically while considering how urgent they were. Most days, I would start and stop and do things to cover up or not think about these triggers. On other days, I would indulge in house chores that keep me busy, not focus on my problems. I remember cooking my favorite food and putting salt in twice without remembering that I had put salt in before, because of which I had to throw away most of the gravy and restart it again. Other times, I focused on ensuring that my task at work was through. I scanned and created daily tasks to ensure I stayed on top of my metrics.

After finishing the house chores, I knew I had to revisit my triggers. Even though I would occasionally run away from reality, I knew that, deep down inside, I wanted to fix my problem. I took some time to regain my strength to put my fear away to focus on my trigger. Nevertheless, the distractions assisted me in separating my feelings and gave me some insight to re-affirm and recollect my thoughts – they allowed me to have the right mindset before working on myself.

Once I confirmed my triggers and understood their urgency, I was able to work hard on them, one at a time. I looked at all the possibilities that led to current and unforeseen triggers and were open-minded to the others that may provoke my emotions in the future. I worked on finding the grounds to develop a manageable plan as I assigned goals and worked upon solving them; I used the analogy of the nursing process as I created a plan for the triggers. While looking at the "PES" acronym, P- problem, E-etiology, and S- systems, I was able to formulate my diagnosis and create both short-term and long-term goals. All my plans were time-oriented, keeping in mind the time frame and ensuring that they were realistic.

In addition, I designed five solvable interventions, choosing the variables that I could control and change. I also looked at the rationales for each intervention and sought to find any scientific perceptive or reasoning. Not just that, but I also considered the consequences of not carrying out any of my selected interventions. Occasionally, I also had to revisit and remove all the interventions that were not solvable as I concluded my evaluation of them.

Once my interventions were sound, I conquered that trigger. I was able to use those interventions to express myself. I would yell out, "Victory is mine!" – I overcame. I knew, at that moment, that I was not going back and dwelling on what made me feel unhappy. As I conquered these battles, I couldn't handle the frustration anymore. I knew I was moving on and on the road to recovery – no more pain or suffering; my tensions were gone. I felt so powerful. And that is how I gained the strength to overcome every obstacle thrown my way. Whenever the triggers to my emotions attempted to interfere in my daily life, I began focusing on the interventions I came up with as my coping mechanism. I prepared myself for the instances when these triggers stepped in again and told myself that certain events would still affect me in the foreseeable future. Most importantly, these interventions were strong enough to assist me to hold still and stay focused.

I also concluded that some triggers to my emotions might never be cured – that I must own them and live peacefully with them. Nevertheless, the interventions I created would continue to serve as a coping methodology and become my go-to whenever needed. They were always kept in handy to depend on them and find my solitude. The interventions not only regulated my emotions but also helped me in my meditation exercises too. Unfortunately, my emotions would still linger around and keep giving me flashbacks, but all of that is just a part of being human. I believe it is more important to have coping strategies and interventions that would come to my aid whenever the triggers begin to intensify.

As I put my interventions into action, I knew it was crucial to begin sustaining them. I reminded myself that once they have been implemented, they become my building blocks and that I must embrace them wholeheartedly. I ensured that these interventions were well-thought-of and eloquent so that it is possible to keep myself from falling apart whenever I feel empty or lost. At times, I would feel the intense pressure to explode, but I took hold of myself and released the choking grip of anxiety constantly hanging on my head. I quickly took hold of my thoughts to free myself from the consuming pressure that was beginning to choke me. There were times when I watched the television and noticed people suffering from negativity in their lives, just like me, and felt empathetic when they cried themselves to sleep dejectedly. I always wished that I could just hand them my interventions or lend a shoulder for support.

I know for a fact that some people are fearful of seeking assistance, the ones suffering and deeply embedded with pessimism. I found myself occasionally thinking about the neighbors living up the block, a couple. I remembered how they took the life of their one and only daughter over harsh circumstances that they were suffering from. It quivers my heart to realize that without proper interventions, people's lives just end tragically – that is not how it is supposed to be.

"When dealing with people, remember you are not dealing with creatures of logic, but creatures of emotion." - Dale Carnegie

Most recently, I learned multiple stories of law enforcement officers who took their own lives due to an immense amount of pressure and stress on their shoulders. This is the archetype of poor coping skills and no interventions to rely upon. It is wrong to assume that everyone lives a happy and satisfied life if you cannot see the suffering of life on their faces. In the society that we live in, people make their way in life while remaining in distress constantly, and those who seem fine may be doped up with pharmacotherapies. These drugs are not effective enough as they often cause side effects that may harm your life in many ways than you can imagine.

During my nursing career, I also encountered a group of patients under my care who were suffering emotionally and using heavy analgesics to escape from their problems. After talking to them in-depth, they confided in me and told me they had no physical pain. The pain they desperately wanted to escape was from past tragic events in their lives; to run away from those feelings, they just wanted to stay knocked out.

Even though these conversations were 100% confidential, I believed that it was my responsibility to convey to these patients the importance of seeking help in the right way, at the right time. At the end of our conversation, they thanked me for looking out for them and ensuring that they look out for themselves too. While I was helping these patients, their stories also prepared me to deal with my own emotions.

Likewise, many other instances in my own family ended tragically. I had never felt as helpless as I did when my sister-in-law took her own life. In her case, she silently suffered from many personal issues and conflicts and did not seek help. It is not possible to always detect the symptoms of depression and stress by just looking at someone's face; hers were concealed quite well during my face-to-face encounters.

Perhaps she may have been forcing herself to live like that, but how long can one keep up a façade for? With her not being around, I recalled the instances when she danced to her favorite music – I still remember how joyful she looked. Nobody could see through the image she was putting up. Thinking back at these events, I reflected upon how

I could have been more effective and efficient in offering my support to others around me. I still ask this question to date: did these horrible events happen in my life? What could have been a better approach for me to adopt? As I continued to refer to my diary, I curated the interventions to match those events. These thoughts do not seem to disappear entirely; some triggers keep reminding me that these events are real and that I cannot alter my past.

Nevertheless, I countered that thought with hopefulness: I still have the chance to control the current and future events. I kept telling myself not to take anyone for granted and perceive that all is well in their lives. Any conversation that I indulged in, I keenly listened to that person and remained sensitive to their issues. As I listened to them, I did not let their emotions overpower mine and immediately sought my interventions whenever it started getting too much.

I tried not to feel overwhelmed while listening to other people, even though I knew my interventions were solid. While working on my interventions, I took into account that listening about and watching the emotions that people suffer from could bring an odd sense of heaviness on my shoulders. I learned this from my mother because she was an astute observer of her surroundings and other people. Whenever I would sit quietly, she would ask me if I had the entire world's problems on my shoulders. One's whole demeanor can tell you several things about their emotion. During this time, I preoccupied myself with only the positive interventions that I implemented and repeated the same approaches each time the flashback of any past traumatic event hit.

While reflecting on my past and the flashbacks I kept on having, I also remember not being true to myself. I did not practice truthful judgment because I did not want to be judged by others. It is pretty unlucky how a selfless person could also feel embarrassed by their own emotions.

This discouraged me and held me back from offering help the society. I still feel the guilt because I could have intervened and done something more to assist the people who were suffering, as many of my colleagues wound me for a piece of advice. I will be more sensitive to any hint thrown at me in the future.

Empowerment

One good thing came out of my struggles: I acquired the courage and strength to empower others and motivate them to talk about their issues. After understanding my own emotions, I learned that I have the power to support others whenever they need help. Nowadays, people need to keep in mind that they can use the resources available for their help.

They can always seek. Even though they may also opt for pharmacological treatment, I firmly believe that they need to read and hear about how the people suffering from personal issues regain their strength. Similarly, they too can adopt the same tools necessary to develop the coping strategies that will help them and eventually help others.

Revitalization

There were times when I felt like I was always running a marathon; I had no energy left in me and always felt lightheaded. My face would remain crumpled up as I sobbed profusely. The feeling of withdrawal and weakness attempted to creep in. I had reserved so much strength for my spiritual interventions and had to revisit and use them to rejuvenate myself. Albeit a hard lesson learned, it is crucial to acknowledge that you must plant enough to reap a lot. I had to wrap my head around the fact that I cannot afford to deplete my energy and always leave a reserve, as my dad would like to say, "left- left." Adopting this strategy as a way of life would benefit anyone who chooses to live through it.

Sharing

I firmly believe that one should always share helpful guidelines with others around them, especially in their day-to-day lives. Just imagine how many lives you could influence and transform if you provided others with tried-and-tested sources of inspiration! I started with my students, who confided in me about their frustrations and struggles in school and at home, too – most of them weren't aware of the sources they should turn to for help. The enlightenment I received from my difficult situations became an excellent service when I assisted my students in developing their coping mechanisms and getting through school. They referred to me as a 'mother-teacher,' and I wanted to act just like one – I would use my direct and positive interventions to build and transform their energy. Through this, I created a bond with my students and a strong, everlasting relationship. Undoubtedly, some would fear me at first, but they, too, would get over it after I nurtured and supported them through encouragement. The push and upliftment I provided strengthened their self-confidence and guided them to focus well and pass their classes with flying colors.

Collaboration

God indeed places some people in your life for specific reasons. When I met my former boss at one of the institutions I taught in, it was so refreshing to click with her immediately. We caught up and began sharing our lives - rejoiced and raptured, knowing that our battles were successful. As I shared some of my experiences, only momentarily, I was teary-eyed. Nevertheless, the conversation took a turn as she boosted my morale and was genuinely proud of me. It astonished me to know that, as professionals, we had encountered such trauma in our lives but did not let it alter our spirits.

The combination of our encounters amalgamated and collaborated to the point where we had our moments in which we could empower each other and build a relationship with other people to embrace a future of upliftment and strength. Together, we hoped that our collaborative vigor would encourage and motivate the people with whom we might come in contact. That not only professional women of color and strong faith, but the entire universe needed to hear our stories so that they can be empowered into moving forward in life and inspire others into doing the same.

CHAPTER 19:

Finding Comfort while Building Myself

After overcoming all of my struggles and fighting my way out of them, I began taking care of my well-being. It is crucial to hold your mental and physical health in the utmost regard and uphold your self-worth and values. I know everyone agrees with that too, but they are all a tad bit murky on the follow-through. There are many self-care strategies out there, and all you need to do is find the ones that complement your lifestyle. If you would like a piece of advice and something to take inspiration from, the following is what I did and followed as a routine to build myself up.

- Finding comfort in who you are is essential, but sometimes you need to change your appearance to feel good about yourself. To do that, I always tried to take good care of not just my body but also my mind and soul. I did that by enhancing my outward appearance altogether; I worked on my hairstyle by adding some highlights, getting bangs after occasional haircuts, and braiding my hair with style. My hair was always a little fuzzy, so I used gel to enhance its look and used hair sprays to hold my messy hair in place. Sometimes, I would also opt for an occasional ponytail because I knew I had a beautiful face cut and could always feel good about myself when it was apparent.

- I treated my face right by getting facials; however, skincare could also be as simple as washing your face before going to bed and after waking up. I practiced skincare, not just for hygiene but also for maintaining healthy and glowing skin. Improving my collection of makeup and lipsticks, I brought a little change and used gloss as well! Not just that, but I also used petroleum jelly to prevent my lips from breaking out and cracking.

- I also liked getting my nails in shape; whenever feasible, I would treat myself to a manicure and pedicure, and sometimes, I would grow them a little or add tips. I ensured that my nails were always clean and well-groomed to prevent them from being chipped.

- I changed my wardrobe by taking inspiration from my profession. I started dressing formally, wearing a jacket, or a slightly fitted sweater, even if I was going to the grocery store or the post office.

- I refrained from wearing sagging and dark clothing. I only wore sweatpants and sweat-tops if I was going to the park, gym, or jogging.

- I put on matching heels, alternating the colors and avoiding black altogether. Matching the heels with my clothes gave me a boost of confidence as I stepped into my new life.

- I added some jewelry to enhance my attire; Only minimalistic, though, because I did not want to choke myself with too much nor wear too much on each hand.

- I added a pocketbook to boost my looks; as I chose a dark outfit, I would always compliment it with a bright or multi-color pocketbook.

It was just as essential to work on my internal self rather than just focusing on looking good on the outside. Looking beautiful and attractive made me feel better about my appearance, but being a pleasant person is salient in anyone's personality. Keeping that in mind and changing my mindset, I reminded myself that I could not continue to carry the same brashness around. Working on a better me, I changed my approach in the way I wanted everyone to see and interact with me.

- I smiled more often. Even on days when I did not have the energy to do so, I put on a fake smile, the way my cousin taught me. Often practicing a pleasant smile in the mirror, I aimed to make this my new public appearance. Additionally, I greeted everyone in the same fashion so that they did not see the wrinkles and blemishes on my face but just a heartfelt and wholesome smile. No matter who the person was, I would meet them the same way even if I did not know them.

- One must always utter good things and stay silent if they have nothing better to say – that became my motto in life. I spoke delicately and eloquently, choosing my vocabulary accordingly and using jargon whenever they were conducive in the surrounding, I would be in. I refrained from speaking loudly and using obscene words, allowing my body language to display and represent my spoken words positively.

- Kindness indeed begins with the understanding that everyone around us is tied up in their struggles. Showing appreciation to the people around me, I began expressing my gratitude after someone would say something gratifying to me or gift me something. If you do not express your thankfulness to someone, how will they know you appreciate them? Adopting the same ideology, I began letting everyone know how much I treasured their existence in my life. I showed respect to everyone, especially the less fortunate, the frail and elderly, and the disabled, by greeting them with kind words always.

- I adopted a strategy to continue my conversations smoothly by using words such as 'Yes, Ma'am,' or 'Yes, Sir,' to demonstrate my admiration and respect for the people around me.

- I learned to consistently turn a blind eye to things that do not concern me or the things that would harm my mental peace. As funny as that sounds, it was helpful to consider myself a local celebrity; my life constituted of my former in-laws watching and reporting every move and aspect of my life. It would bother me initially, but then I realized that most of the information was just a blatant lie. In a way, it was hilarious that they were wasting their time gossiping about me while I was progressing into a strong, empowered woman.

Restoring My Energy

Leaders like you and I need to maintain their energy, conserving it and spending it on vital avenues only. The same energy would provide us with the endurance to remain productive and achieve great things in life. I would get myself going and retain my vitality through a few habits that worked like a charm.

- *A healthy and balanced diet*: I created a mental menu that consisted of a balanced diet, blending smoothies in the morning and using them as a quick form of energy. The remainder of my meals consisted of a balanced diet; at times, I would consume starches in larger quantities, but soon, I realized that my weight was stagnant, so I began lessening the starches and eating more veggies.

- *Engaging in exercise therapy*: I had scheduled arrangements with a personal trainer, but on the other days, I would participate in routine exercises through the stair-climber, weights, and the treadmill. I also walked for miles around the neighborhood and, at times, the nearby parks.

- *Music therapy*: soft harmonies in music were always my escape. I always sang and danced to some of my favorite songs, and other songs with meaningful lyrics would allow me to focus on the words and the tunes. As the profound words coincided with my feelings, I would tune them up and find my comfort in knowing that someone else could relate to me too.

Rearranging My Circle

I maintained communication with everyone around me, but I

developed a stronger bond with those who understood what I was going through and supported me emotionally. Most of these people were educated colleagues who stood by me through my pain and told me that I am an independent woman and will find my way out soon. However, others told me to hold on, but I believe that was out of their benefit. Some also told me to run away, as they were fearful for my life. I continued being me but eased off on dinners and social meetings with most of them. We would occasionally chat whenever they required medical advice or during death to offer condolences, but most of these communications were through text messages. However, I ensured that I kept in close contact with my new church's pastor and often sought prayers over there.

Personalizing My Space

The small guest room that I moved into was near the main bedroom, which was also my marital room. I redecorated the windows with light-colored curtains so that my room would be brighter, and I would use the beaming sunshine rays to add a sparkle to my life. Not only this, but I removed all the wall décor and left the wall bare; for me, this represented that all my sorrows had finally vanished. The room was filled with books and papers with my computer on the side to represent a change in priorities as I look forward to a new life – and betterment in my career.

Preventing self-destruction

I detached myself from anyone that would pull me apart and instead offered nothing to motivate me. Engaging myself with individuals who stimulated and uplifted me to strive for excellence improved my mood significantly. These individuals encouraged me to use my leadership skills to become an entrepreneur and directed me to a suitable business path.

Freeing Myself

After accomplishing everything mentioned above, I began feeling like myself again. I disconnected from all the fallacies people had to say about me, starting to 'love me and do me.' I felt free; as though the heaviness on my chest was lifted, the bundle of pain and sorrow in my life were gone. I was delighted in myself for living bravely and remaining steadfast despite everything that happened – I was so sure that nothing could bring me down anymore.

Speaking Up

Utilizing my freedom of speech, I started owning everything I would say. I corrected and confronted everyone spreading false information about my family and me. Without having anything to fear, I spoke to my former spouse about his extramarital relationship. Although it did cause a huge disagreement and a more significant rift between us, at least it was finally off of my chest. I started letting people know my point of view immediately, whether directly or indirectly. The ability to express myself made me realize what works for me and what does not – the latter had no place in my life anymore.

EPILOGUE

I realized that it was time to say goodbye to my marriage after my former spouse stopped talking to me for two years and became calling me every derogatory name in history. During this time, my integrity was demolished, and I felt hopeless. I lost faith in him and realized that my best friend was now my enemy.

I would previously describe our relationship as a fairytale love story, then. When he finally called me a 'wicked witch,' for whom he 'would never beg for,' I was so afraid to know that I could never sleep with or love this man ever again. I was at a loss of words and teary-eyed when I stepped outside for a walk in the neighborhood and called my former bother-in-law.

Unsure of why, but I believed that I would receive some words of support or comfort from him – I was wrong. As I told him about the hurtful phrases and vented about my intentions for a divorce, he said that he would support his brother wholeheartedly, even if my former spouse was wrong.

It was my naivety to look up to this family as my very own. I was under the assumption that what we had was incomparable. I couldn't reach out to his mother because she suddenly started talking to me differently, saying things that I never expected from her – albeit in a softer tone. The speeches she gave me were full of expression, disorienting me completely, to the point where I had to ask her why she spoke like a hypocrite. That was a massive shift from all the fun and laughter we shared – but perhaps, it was all a façade.

At this point, my former spouse and most of his family members maliciously began destroying my integrity by telling tales. I felt the tension, the division, and the prior love for a motherless girl was no longer there; I had to wave goodbye. Standing up for myself when I had nobody else, I went to the courthouse and filed for my divorce – we had a snowstorm that day, but nothing in this universe could come in my way once I had made up my mind.

To be fair, only for the sake of our beloved kids, Mary and Melanie, I was not planning to leave our family home until they were finished with school. I was hoping that they flourish in the neighborhood they were familiar with and get to be with their childhood friends.

I wanted them to continue their daily activities, being parented by both of us collectively. To keep things cordial, I would lock myself into the tiny, blue-painted guest room whenever my former husband was home. I cooked and completed the chores in his absence, greeting the kids more often, so they believe that I am doing well – that they do not need to worry about me and focus on themselves.

I locked myself into that room whenever I was feeling depressed, going to my computer searching for a home in South Jersey. I went through some potential houses with the girls, but they were either very pricey or not in good condition. I also worried about my credit score since I had previously lost two of my houses. Nevertheless, during my search, I also came across an advertisement for online dating; feeling lonely, I signed up and found some interesting men. However, my luck was charmed when I met the love of my life on Zoosk, who is also my current husband. On January 18th, 2015, I grabbed my clothes from the closet, some from my drawer, and opened the wall unit to grab all the important documents. Afterward, I shouted for my daughter to grab all of her school belongings and some clothes as I waved goodbye to my marital home at 522 Hory Street, Roselle, New Jersey, and headed to join my boyfriend in Chestnut Ridge, New York.

As I swiftly walked to load my car, I waved my final goodbye to the antique furniture, linens, pots, and dishes that I acquired in the past eighteen years and the remainder of my clothes. I took another look at my beautiful wall décor and the crystal standing, which would forever be deserted in the China cabinet. I inhaled the aroma of my plants hanging in the bay window before exiting, once and for all.

From the loudness of my former husband's voice, the way he was screaming at me, and his anger and bitterness towards me, I knew that the night might not end well. Although my former husband and I shared our marital home, we were in separate bedrooms until the house got sold. I was petrified, but I knew I had to immediately remove myself and my daughter from his emotionally abusive behavior. By this time, I was living in a constant state of fear after being tormented for the past three years. As I stepped my feet into the car, attached my seat belt, and put my car in reverse, I glanced at the house number as the waterworks began to flow. While I drove out of Hory street, I waved goodbye to the neighborhood in silence. Even though my recent memories left a sour taste in my mouth, I was reminiscing about the good times I had spent over there. But I had to close that chapter and move on. It was for the greater good. I reached my boyfriend's home at about 9 p.m. while he was at work and called him to surprise him with the news. His reaction is one that I can never forget: he said to me that he was the happiest man on earth, asking me what took me so long.

My lifelong experiences up till the tortuous ending of my previous marriage, the persecutions I endured, along with the persuasion of my family and friends, motivated me to share my stories with you all.

I hope they inspire all of you who are suffering emotionally and are feeling lost, knowing that there is still hope. After reading my stories, let your strength ascend. Have faith in yourself. Nobody can change your life if you do not change it yourself. Keep pulling through, for life has great things planned for you.

I believe in you.

Believe in yourself, too.

To You

I felt the drive to motivate the young and middle-aged men and women, especially the women: you no longer have to struggle. There is hope. You must first realize that you are suffering as I did and decide if you want to overcome or if you want to continue suffering. After reading this book, I hope it will strengthen you to take a leap of faith to move forward and be driven by the steps I took. Grab your pen and paper and start your journey to recovery. You must also consider that no one wins a game by moving forward alone. Sometimes, you may have to take baby steps, and while doing that, you may creep backward before taking the step forward. Being ready to take control of your life and changing for the greater good is the most significant step.

You may feel lost at first and have many questions to ask yourself. There will be many times when you may have doubts like I did. The feelings of discouragement will make things undesirable, and this feeling might prevail, but only if you let them. Additionally, you may feel this way because it is easier to give up. Remember: you are designed to make mistakes. Some of these mistakes will destroy your enthusiasm. You may also take a long time to recover or come to that point of realization, but do not feel like you are going backward or are too engulfed in your struggles.

Certain moods may come to teach you and inspire you, while others may simplify the path that you follow next. Each day, you will be stronger and wiser than the day before. Bear in mind: you cannot go back and undo what has already been done, but you can pick up the pieces and move on. Once you have adopted this mindset, believe me, you can move mountains. If you are spiritual, read Philippians 4:6-7. Be anxious over nothing. Through prayers and supplication, request God to guard your heart and mind through His benevolence, for He is omnipotence and omniscience. Keep in mind, always, that *"the Lord is a mighty tower where his people can run for safety."* (Proverbs 18:10).

www.ingramcontent.com/pod-product-compliance
Lightning Source LLC
Chambersburg PA
CBHW020608160726
47991CB00002BA/687